The Great Songwriters of Hollywood

Also by WARREN CRAIG:

Sweet and Lowdown

The Great Songwriters of Hollywood

Warren Craig

San Diego • New York

A. S. Barnes & Company, Inc.

In London:

The Tantivy Press

For Jim and Josh

The Great Songwriters of Hollywood text copyright ©1980 by Warren Craig
A. S. Barnes and Co., Inc.

The Tantivy Press
Magdalen House
136-148 Tooley Street
London, SE1 2TT, England

First Edition
Manufactured in the United States of America
For information write to A. S. Barnes and Company, Inc.,
P.O. Box 3051, San Diego, CA 92038

Library of Congress Cataloging in Publication Data

Craig, Warren, 1924-
   The great songwriters of Hollywood.

   Includes lists of songs.
   Includes index.
   1.   Composers—California—Hollywood—Biography.
2.   Librettists—California—Hollywood—Biography.
3.   Moving-picture music—History and criticism.
4.   Musical revue, comedy, etc.—United States.
I.   Title.
ML390.C86   784.5′0092′2   [B]   79-87793
ISBN 0-498-02439-3

   1   2   3   4   5   6   7   8   9   84   83   82   81   80

Contents

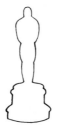

2131117

Foreword

I was there . . . and I still am.

Hollywood has been my home for nearly fifty years—almost from the moment motion pictures found a voice and began to talk. There were many of us here, lyricists and composers writing words and music for the singing stars. But unlike our colleagues, the greats of the Broadway musical theater, we never got our names above the titles; that place went to the stars or occasionally to a producer or director. We were generally considered part of the equipment: a song-composing machine expected to turn out not just songs, but "hits" at the drop of a whole note, tailored to the style of a certain performer. And after the songs had been created, like as not we were taken off salary!

Yes, it wasn't all beer and pretzels in a bed of roses. There were difficulties, misunderstandings, arguments, politics, and intrigues, but then I suppose every job carries those hazards. And there were plenty of bright spots to even things out. How could I forget the first viewing of the final screen version of the tremendous production number Busby Berkeley concocted based on Al Dubin's and my unpretentious rhythm song "Lullaby of Broadway"? Who could forget the beautifully warm and tender way Alice Faye sang "You'll Never Know" or the way Judy Garland belted out "On the Atchison, Topeka and the Santa Fe" in that wild West setting in *The Harvey Girls?*

It all went so fast. Almost before we knew it, television had replaced the old Hollywood scene. But now Warren Craig has gathered all this information about those of us who worked in films and presented it in this book. I found great pleasure in going through the material, remembering again the many great songs of the thirties, forties, and fifties, and recalling the other composers and lyricists who created them—many of them my personal friends and many of them now gone. Here at last is a book that names names and lists songs. After all, if it hadn't been for us songwriters and our songs, there wouldn't have been any film musicals, would there? We are all indebted to Mr. Craig for presenting us and our work in such a splendid book.

Looking back over it all—the good, the bad, the indifferent—I'm very glad I was there.

Harry Warren
Beverly Hills
November 1978

Acknowledgments

The author wishes to thank the following people for their assistance: Dr. David Morton, Lucille Meyers, Hilda Schneider, Marshall Robbins, Ray Evans, Peggy O'Brien, and Arthur Hamilton.

Unless noted otherwise, the photographs of composers and lyricists are by the courtesy of the artists. All sheet music covers were furnished by the UCLA Archive of Popular American Music.

Introduction

The musical is the only type of movie entertainment at which the American film industry has excelled. Foreign cinemamakers have produced dramas, comedies, and costume epics that have equaled and even surpassed the efforts of Hollywood, but none of them has mastered the art of the screen musical. From the history-making moment when Al Jolson sang to moviegoers in *The Jazz Singer* in 1927 through such memorable productions as *Broadway Melody, Forty-Second Street, Top Hat, The Great Ziegfeld, Goldwyn Follies, Star Spangled Rhythm, Cover Girl, State Fair, Romance on the High Seas, Easter Parade, Seven Brides for Seven Brothers,* and *Thoroughly Modern Millie,* foreign and domestic audiences alike have relied on American ingenuity for the best musicals ever put on film.

Popular songs became an integral part of film exhibition during the days of the nickelodeons. Live entertainers sang the newest hits and urged the audience to join in the chorus, assisting them with slides projected on the screen. It soon became apparent that contemporary music could be used to advertise silent movies. Among the first hit songs associated with a screen presentation was "Mickey" written to publicize Mabel Normand's 1918 film of that title. It was followed by "Charmaine," "My Dream of the Big Parade" and "Diane" used to tout the releases of *What Price Glory?, The Big Parade,* and *Seventh Heaven.* But it remained for the addition of sound to films to change popular songs from a useful accessory of the motion picture business to one of its most vital elements. Realizing that the production of hundreds of talking motion pictures annually would consume enormous amounts of popular

music, the studios began accumulating music publishing houses. Within a few short years, Hollywood had absorbed Tin Pan Alley.

Beginning in 1928, every popular song composer or lyricist of any reputation whatever eventually found himself on the payroll of a film studio. The Broadway theater saw most of its talented songwriters head for California, many of them never to return. The motion picture industry cornered the market on songwriters and held a virtual monopoly on their services for more than two decades.

Among Hollywood's initial attempts at incorporating popular songs into motion pictures were all-star revues featuring most of a studio's contract players. The revues included Warner Brothers' *Show of Shows* with Alice White, Ben Turpin, Louise Fazenda, Richard Barthelmess, Dolores Costello, Loretta Young, Patsy Ruth Miller, Lila Lee, Myrna Loy, Chester Morris, Sally Eilers, John Barrymore, and Rin Tin Tin; Metro-Goldwyn-Mayer's *Hollywood Revue of 1929* with Marion Davies, Norma Shearer, Joan Crawford, Conrad Nagel, Jack Benny, Lionel Barrymore, Laurel and Hardy, John Gilbert, William Haines, Buster Keaton, Marie Dressler, and Polly Moran; and *Paramount on Parade* with Maurice Chevalier, Nancy Carroll, Richard Arlen, Clara Bow, Gary Cooper, Kay Francis, Helen Kane, and Jack Oakie. Adaptations of Broadway musicals for the sound screen included *Sally, Little Johnny Jones, The Desert Song, So Long, Letty* and *Rio Rita.* Among the early musicals written especially for motion pictures were *Applause, Sunny Side Up, Broadway Melody, Playboy of Paris, The Singing Fool,* and *Puttin' on the*

11

Ritz. The immobility of the sound camera defeated attempts at originality, and the musical numbers in these films were presented as though they were being performed on a stage with the movie patrons viewing the performance from the normal position of a theater audience. Hollywood finally succeeded in flooding the market with hundreds of musicals during the early thirties. When the novelty of sound for its own sake wore off, audiences tired of watching the static production numbers.

The man responsible for bringing back the Hollywood musical was Busby Berkeley who exercised his imagination to extremes undreamed of by other directors. With cameras mounted on the floor and ceiling, he arranged his dancers in geometric patterns while they performed calisthenics in rhythm to music. Berkeley's cameras recorded the movement of neon violins, grand pianos, and human harps. People and furniture alike exploded into bits, only to be reassembled for the next chorus of the song.

Berkeley began hitting his stride in 1933 with the Warner Brothers releases *Forty-Second Street, Footlight Parade,* and *Gold Diggers of 1933.* Their success resulted in other major studios rushing musicals into production. RKO featured Fred Astaire and Ginger Rogers in *Flying Down to Rio;* Fox presented Alice Faye in *George White's Scandals;* Paramount began a series of campus musicals: *College Humor, College Rhythm, College Holiday,* and *College Scandal.* MGM cast dramatic stars Joan Crawford in *Dancing Lady* and Jean Harlow in *Reckless.* In 1936, the art of the screen musical reached new heights in Metro's spectacular *The Great Ziegfeld.* That same year, a new dimension was added to feature-length musicals when *The Dancing Pirate* was filmed in the newly perfected Technicolor process. The foremost producer of musicals, Warner Brothers, left the field toward the end of the thirties to concentrate on dramas with current themes frequently dealing with the war in Europe.

The United States' involvement in World War II in 1942 brought a resurgence of screen musicals. Motion pictures were the main form of entertainment for overseas troops. Soldiers, sailors, and marines delighted in topical musicals, such as *Here Come the Waves, Hollywood Canteen, Anchors Aweigh,* and *Follow the Boys,* and period musicals, such as *Sweet Rosie O'Grady, Meet Me in St. Louis, Shine on Harvest Moon,* and *Wabash Avenue.* Musical stars Betty Grable and Rita Hayworth vied for the title of World War II's most popular pin-up girl.

After the armistice in 1945, patrons continued to flock to the cinema to see Esther Williams in *This Time for Keeps,* Betty Hutton in *Perils of Pauline,* Jane Powell in *Two Weeks with Love,* and June Allyson in *Good News.* But the days of Hollywood musicals were numbered. In 1948, Americans began buying large quantities of television sets and viewing movies in their living rooms. Hollywood had one remaining major advantage—color. During the early fifties, film musicals, such as *Take Me Out to the Ball Game, Annie Get Your Gun, My Blue Heaven,* and *April Love* were box office bonanzas. But when the price of a color television set came within the reach of the average citizen, the death knell was sounded for the Hollywood song and dance epics. Americans could now watch musical films, variety shows, and spectaculars in living color, paying only the price of frequent interruptions by pitchmen.

Screen musicals always involved the work of the same artisans required to create any type of motion picture: scenario writers, directors, actors, cameramen, and set and costume designers. What made them unique were the talents of the men—and occasional women—responsible for the music in musicals— Hollywood's popular song writers! Although their songs were partly responsible for the success of the films on which they worked, these composers and lyricists are almost as unknown to the general public as the electricians, carpenters, and set painters who also labored outside of camera range. Although countless moviegoers left their local cinemas humming "We're in the Money," "I'm in the Mood for Love," "Thanks for the Memory," and "Swinging on a Star," few were aware that the songs were written by composers Harry Warren, Jimmy McHugh, Ralph Rainger, and James Van Heusen, and lyricists Al Dubin, Dorothy Fields, Leo Robin, and Johnny Burke. Yet the motion picture musical would never have developed without the talents of such writers. This book documents the careers of the greatest of them.

Two hundred and fifty-four songs have competed for the Academy of Motion Picture Arts and Sciences Best Song award since it was implemented in 1934. The first statuettes were presented to composer Con Conrad and lyricist Herbert Magidson for "The Continental" introduced in *The Gay Divorcee*. The thirty-two composers and lyricists selected for this book received a total of 214 nominations for Hollywood's highest honor. By 1978, these artists had won twenty-five of the possible forty-four Best Song Oscars. All of them have been inducted into the Songwriters' Hall of Fame.

The composers and lyricists included in these pages are those who contributed substantially to motion pictures throughout their lifetimes. Although many of them were also successful in writing for the legitimate theater, only their work for films is of concern here. Several noted Broadway songwriters, such as Cole Porter, George Gershwin, and Richard Rodgers, have been omitted from this study. The motion pictures on which such artists worked were outstanding, but their excursions into the celluloid medium were relatively infrequent.

Irving Berlin

When Al Jolson sang to movie audiences in October of 1927, one of the numbers he selected was written by the most successful popular song writer in American history. The song was "Blue Skies" with music and lyrics by Irving Berlin. The composition had been featured in the 1926 Broadway musical *Betsy* and was already a hit when it was interpolated by Jolson into *The Jazz Singer*.

Irving Berlin was 39 years old when sound was introduced in films. His family had come to the United States from Russia in the 1890's and settled on New York City's East Side. He ran away from home at the age of 14. While employed as a singing waiter, he wrote the words for his first song "Marie from Sunny Italy" in 1907. His association with Broadway began the following year when he placed a song in the 1908 musical comedy *The Boys and Betty*. Within two years, Berlin was appearing in vaudeville at the Palace Theatre and singing and dancing in the revue *Up and Down Broadway* which featured two numbers with lyrics by the aspiring songwriter. His aspirations were fully realized in 1911 when variety star Emma Carus performed a song with both music and lyrics by Berlin during an engagement in Chicago. The number was "Alexander's Ragtime Band" and it swept the country. During the next six years, Berlin's work was heard in sixteen stage musicals, and he wrote the music and lyrics for such successful songs as "When the Midnight Choo-Choo Leaves for Alabam'," "When I Lost You," "Play a Simple Melody," "I Want to Go Back to Michigan," and "I Love a Piano."

Berlin enlisted in the Army in 1917 but sat out World War I at Camp Upton. While in the service, he assembled an all-soldier revue in which he sang his classic "Oh, How I Hate to Get Up in the Morning." After the armistice, he became a regular contributor to Florenz Ziegfeld's annual *Follies* and then decided to create his own revue series. In conjunction with producer Sam H. Harris, Berlin financed the construction of the million dollar Music Box Theatre in which the first *Music Box Revue* opened in 1921. Berlin composed "Say It with Music" as the theme for his revue, which was presented annually through 1924. By the time "Blue Skies" was introduced to motion picture audiences in 1927, Berlin's catalog of hit songs had been expanded to include "A Pretty Girl Is Like a Melody," "All by Myself," "Lazy," "What'll I Do?," "All Alone," "Always," and "(You Forgot to) Remember."

Irving Berlin began providing original material for films in 1928 when his composition "Marie" was featured in *The Awakening* starring Vilma Banky. Miss Banky's voice was considered unsuitable for the sound cameras, and her Hollywood career came to an end, but Berlin went on to become the most successful writer of both music and lyrics in screen history. Among his activities the next year were the first all-Negro "talkie" *Hallelujah* and *The Cocoanuts*, in which the four Marx Brothers made their film debut. In 1930, he created the scores for *Mammy* starring Al Jolson and *Puttin' on the Ritz* in which Broadway veteran Harry Richman appeared with Joan Bennett. After providing the title song for Douglas Fairbanks' 1931 release *Reaching for the Moon*, Berlin left the Hollywood scene to supply Broadway with such memorable compositions as "Let's Have Another Cup of Coffee," "Soft Lights and Sweet Music," "Heat Wave," and "Easter Parade."

Unlike most songwriters who were assigned by their studios to work on as many as a dozen motion pictures a year, Berlin's reputation as the dean of popular music composers enabled him to be selective about his projects. While he had been concentrating on musicals for the legitimate theater, RKO (Radio-Keith-Orpheum) Studio had launched the film careers of a new song and dance team named Fred Astaire and Ginger Rogers in the 1933 release *Flying Down to Rio*. The enthusiastic reception given the team by both the public and the critics led to their appearance the next year in *The Gay Divorcee*. The scores for Rogers and Astaire's first two offerings were by such top songwriters as Gus Kahn, Vincent Youmans, Edward Eliscu, Cole Porter, Mack Gordon, Harry Revel, Con Conrad, and Herbert Magidson. RKO wanted Irving Berlin as its composer-lyricist for Rogers and Astaire's next musical, and the offer brought Berlin back to the West Coast. The score he created for *Top Hat* was the first of his Hollywood blockbusters. His songs "Isn't This a Lovely Day?" "No Strings," and "Top Hat, White Tie and Tails" each placed on the weekly broadcasts of "Your Hit Parade" that was the national barometer of song popularity. The biggest hit from *Top Hat* was "Cheek to Cheek," which captured the "Hit Parade's" number one spot and was nominated for the 1935 Best Song Oscar. Berlin remained with RKO for a second Rogers and Astaire vehicle titled *Follow the Fleet* in which the "Hit Parade" favorites "Let Yourself Go," "I'm Putting All My Eggs in One Basket," and "Let's Face the Music and Dance" were introduced. After *Follow the Fleet*, Berlin moved to the Twentieth Century-Fox lot to work on *On the Avenue* featuring Alice Faye, Dick Powell, Madeleine Carroll, and the Ritz Brothers. His third film in as many years produced four more compositions that made "Your Hit Parade" broadcasts: "Slumming on Park Avenue," "You're Laughing at Me," "I've Got My Love to Keep Me Warm," and another number one song—"This Year's Kisses." Berlin functioned as the composer and lyricist on two more musicals for Twentieth Century-Fox and another Rogers and Astaire film at RKO. His efforts for all three films brought him Academy Award nominations. Both "Now It Can Be Told" from *Alexander's Ragtime Band* and "Change Partners" from *Carefree* vied for the 1938 Best Song Oscar, and "I Poured My Heart into a Song" was a contender in 1939.

When the United States entered World War II, Irving Berlin again assembled an all-soldier revue. *This Is the Army* opened on Broadway on Independence Day in 1942. The composer donated his royalties from the show to Army Emergency Relief, and it eventually added ten million dollars to the fund. The profits from his song "I Threw a Kiss in the Ocean" went to the Navy Relief Fund. While *This Is the Army* entertained theater audiences both at home and abroad, movie fans enjoyed one of the first hit screen musicals of the war years— Irving Berlin's *Holiday Inn* produced by Paramount. The picture concerned two song and dance men (Bing Crosby and Fred Astaire) who operated a hotel and cabaret that opened only on holidays. The cabaret's floor show featured a special song written to celebrate the particular holiday. *Holiday Inn* was a milestone in Berlin's career when his melody celebrating Christmas proved to be one of the biggest moneymakers in popular music history. The song "White Christmas" has sold over 117 million records. The composer has stated that he wouldn't sell his copyright to the song for a million dollars. The number holds the record for the most appearances on "Your Hit Parade," having been among the ten top tunes thirty-two times. "White Christmas" was selected as the Best Song of 1942.

Holiday Inn was Berlin's last motion picture for the duration. After the war, he captivated Broadway with his long-run hit *Annie Get Your Gun* and signed with Paramount for another Bing Crosby and Fred Astaire musical, *Blue Skies*. Its' score brought him a 1946 Oscar nomination for "You Keep Coming Back like a Song." Two years later, Metro-Goldwyn-Mayer presented Judy Garland and Fred Astaire in Irving Berlin's *Easter Parade*.

Berlin celebrated his sixty-second birthday in 1950 with another stage success *Call Me Madam*. The remainder of his career saw a sharp reduction in his professional activity. He wrote songs for two more film musicals in 1954: *There's No Business like Show Business* and *White Christmas*, which featured the seventh of his Oscar-nominated songs "Count Your Blessings instead of Sheep." Irving Berlin said goodbye to Hollywood with his title song for the 1957 dramatic film *Sayonara*, which was actually written for an unproduced Broadway musical.

Among the many honors bestowed on Irving Berlin during the almost sixty years of his active career have been a gold medal from the United States Congress for his song "God Bless America" and a Medal of Freedom awarded by President Gerald Ford in 1977. Another of the great songwriters of Hollywood, Jerome Kern, once wrote, "Irving Berlin has no place in American music—he is American music."

1928	THE AWAKENING	Marie	1938	ALEXANDER'S RAGTIME BAND	Now It Can Be Told
					My Walking Stick
1929	LADY OF THE PAVEMENTS	Where Is the Song of Songs for Me?			Marching Along with Time
	HALLELUJAH	Waiting at the End of the Road		CAREFREE	Change Partners
					I Used to Be Color Blind
		Swanee Shuffle			The Yam
					The Night Is Filled with Music
	COQUETTE	Coquette			
	THE COCOANUTS	When My Dreams Come True	1939	SECOND FIDDLE	I Poured My Heart into a Song
					I'm Sorry for Myself
1930	MAMMY	Let Me Sing and I'm Happy			Back to Back
		To My Mammy			When Winter Comes
		(Across the Breakfast Table) Looking at You			An Old-Fashioned Tune Always Is New
		Knights of the Road			The Song of the Metronome
	PUTTIN' ON THE RITZ	Puttin' on the Ritz	1942	HOLIDAY INN	White Christmas
		With You			Be Careful, It's My Heart
		Alice in Wonderland			Happy Holiday
1931	REACHING FOR THE MOON	Reaching for the Moon			I've Got Plenty to Be Thankful For
		When the Folks High Up Do the New Lowdown			Song of Freedom
					Let's Start the New Year Right
1935	TOP HAT	Cheek to Cheek			You're Easy to Dance With
		Isn't This a Lovely Day?			Abraham
		The Piccolino			Holiday Inn
		No Strings (I'm Fancy Free)			I Can't Tell a Lie
		Top Hat, White Tie and Tails			I'll Capture Your Heart Singing
1936	FOLLOW THE FLEET	Let Yourself Go			Let's Say It with Firecrackers
		Let's Face the Music and Dance			
		We Saw the Sea	1946	BLUE SKIES	You Keep Coming Back Like a Song
		I'm Putting All My Eggs in One Basket			A Couple of Song and Dance Men
		Get Thee Behind Me, Satan			A Serenade to an Old-Fashioned Girl
		But Where Are You?			Getting Nowhere
		I'd Rather Lead a Band			
1937	ON THE AVENUE	I've Got My Love to Keep Me Warm	1948	EASTER PARADE	It Only Happens When I Dance with You
		This Year's Kisses			Steppin' Out with My Baby
		Slumming on Park Avenue			A Fella with an Umbrella
		He Ain't Got Rhythm			A Couple of Swells
		You're Laughing at Me			Better Luck Next Time
		The Girl on the Police Gazette			Happy Easter
					Drum Crazy

1954	WHITE CHRISTMAS	Count Your Blessings Instead of Sheep		THERE'S NO BUSINESS LIKE SHOW BUSINESS	A Sailor's Not a Sailor A Man Chases a Girl
		The Best Things Happen While You're Dancing	1957	SAYONARA	Sayonara
		Choreography			
		Gee, I Wish I Was Back in the Army			
		The Old Man			
		Love, You Didn't Do Right by Me			
		Sisters			
		Snow			
		What Can You Do with a General?			

Second Fiddle (Twentieth Century-Fox, 1939).
Collectors Book Store, Hollywood, CA.

Courtesy of the UCLA Archive of Popular American Music

Nacio Herb Brown

While shopping for composers to supply melodies for their new sound musicals, most studios looked for already established talent—preferably tunesmiths with experience in the Broadway theater. Metro-Goldwyn-Mayer was an exception. The man it engaged to write the score for its first major musical was better known in the clothing business than in the songwriting profession. Although he showed promise as a composer, writing music was Nacio Herb Brown's avocation when MGM placed him under contract.

Brown's father was a New Mexico law enforcement officer who relocated his family in Los Angeles in 1904. The boy learned to play the piano and violin while a student at Manual Arts High School. After graduation, he worked as an accompanist for vaudeville performers. He then decided against a career in show business and opened a retail store where he supplied custom-tailored clothes for some of Hollywood's better-dressed silent screen stars. He also sold Southern California real estate. Brown's true love was songwriting, and he used his clothing establishment to gain a foothold in Tin Pan Alley. He persuaded band leaders appearing in local hotels to perform his music in exchange for custom made suits. By this means, he succeeded in having his song "Coral Sea" published in 1920. It was followed by "When Buddha Smiles" in 1921 and "The Hoodoo Man" in 1924. His work impressed the producers of a stage musical who used his instrumental composition "The Doll Dance" in the 1927 offering *The Hollywood Music Box Revue*. "The Doll Dance" became a favorite with dance orchestras throughout the nation. These few successes were the total of Nacio Herb Brown's experience as a popular song writer when he signed his contract with Hollywood's biggest studio.

MGM's major entry into the field of screen musicals with original stories was *Broadway Melody* starring Bessie Love, Charles King, and Anita Page. The studio's gamble on its virtually unknown composer paid off immediately when his score produced three hits: "You Were Meant for Me," "Broadway Melody," and "The Wedding of the Painted Doll." The picture had its Hollywood premiere at Grauman's Chinese Theatre where it played to packed houses for weeks. The newly formed Academy of Motion Picture Arts and Sciences selected *Broadway Melody* as the Best Picture of 1929.

His first year at Metro was a busy one for the ex-haberdasher. Brown's classic "Singin' in the Rain" was heard in *Hollywood Revue of 1929*, and he provided melodies for three of the studio's biggest stars: "Blondy" for Marion Davies in *Marianne*, "Pagan Love Song" for Ramon Navarro's *The Pagan*, and "Chant of the Jungle" for Joan Crawford in *Untamed*. In 1930, he added "Should I?" and "The Moon Is Low" to his catalog of hit film songs. In addition to composing, Brown occasionally indulged in lyric writing and assisted Gordon Clifford with the words for their composition "Paradise," which sultry Pola Negri introduced in the 1932 release *A Woman Commands*. The following year, MGM borrowed Paramount's new musical star Bing Crosby to appear opposite Marion Davies in the Hearst Cosmopolitan production *Going Hollywood*. Almost every song in Brown's score was a national favorite, including "Temptation" which became a popular music standard.

Nacio Herb Brown remained under exclusive contract to MGM for ten years during which his melodies were performed by such top box office stars as Allan Jones, Jeanette MacDonald, Judy Garland, Mickey Rooney, and Eleanor Powell. His songs "Broadway Rhythm," "I've Got a Feelin' You're Foolin'," "Would You," "Yours and Mine," and "Good Morning" all made "Your Hit Parade" broadcasts of the ten top tunes from Maine to California, and "You Are My Lucky Star" and "Alone" were leaders on the weekly surveys. During the last decade of his career, Brown alternated between his home studio and Twentieth Century-Fox composing for such films as *Ziegfeld Girl, Wintertime, Greenwich Village,* and *The Kissing Bandit.*

One of the most memorable in the long line of MGM screen musicals was *Singin' in the Rain* starring Gene Kelly, Debbie Reynolds, and Donald O'Connor. The score for the film consisted almost entirely of the hit songs written by Brown and lyricist Arthur Freed from 1929 through 1939. *Singin' in the Rain* was released in 1952. Nacio Herb Brown died twelve years later at the age of 68. Despite his phenomenal contributions to the art of the screen musical, Brown is one of Hollywood's great songwriters whose melodies were never honored with Academy Award nominations.

1929	BROADWAY MELODY	Broadway Melody You Were Meant for Me The Wedding of the Painted Doll The Love Boat Boy Friend Harmony Babies from Melody Lane
	HOLLYWOOD REVUE OF 1929	Singin' in the Rain Tommy Atkins on Parade
	THE PAGAN	Pagan Love Song
	UNTAMED	Chant of the Jungle
	MARIANNE	Blondy
1930	LORD BYRON OF BROADWAY	Should I The Woman in the Shoe A Bundle of Old Love Letters Only Love Is Real
	MONTANA MOON	The Moon Is Low
	WHOOPEE	I'll Still Belong to You
	ONE HEAVENLY NIGHT	Heavenly Night
	GOOD NEWS	If You're Not Kissing Me Football
1932	A WOMAN COMMANDS	Paradise Promise You'll Remember Me
1933	THE BARBARIAN	Love Songs of the Nile
	STAGE MOTHER	Beautiful Girl I'm Dancing on a Rainbow
	GOING HOLLYWOOD	Temptation After Sundown We'll Make Hay While the Sun Shines Our Big Love Scene Going Hollywood Cinderella's Fella
	HOLD YOUR MAN	Hold Your Man
	PEG O' MY HEART	I'll Remember Only You
1934	SADIE MCKEE	All I Do Is Dream of You Please Make Me Care

	STUDENT TOUR	A New Moon Is Over My Shoulder From Now On The Carlo Snake Dance By the Taj Mahal Fight 'em American Bolero
	HOLLYWOOD PARTY	Hot Chocolate Soldiers
	HIDEOUT	The Dream Was So Beautiful
	RIPTIDE	We're Together Again
1935	BROADWAY MELODY OF 1936	You Are My Lucky Star Broadway Rhythm I've Got a Feelin' You're Foolin' On a Sunday Afternoon Sing before Breakfast
	A NIGHT AT THE OPERA	Alone
	CHINA SEAS	China Seas
1936	SAN FRANCISCO	Would You
	AFTER THE THIN MAN	Smoke Dreams
	THE DEVIL IS A SISSY	Say "Ah!"
1937	BROADWAY MELODY OF 1938	Yours and Mine I'm Feelin' Like a Million Everybody Sing Sun Showers Your Broadway and Mine Get a Pair of New Shoes Follow in My Footsteps
1939	BABES IN ARMS	Good Morning
	THE ICE FOLLIES OF 1939	Something's Gotta Happen Soon
1940	TWO GIRLS ON BROADWAY	My Wonderful One, Let's Dance
1941	ZIEGFELD GIRL	You Stepped Out of a Dream
1943	WINTERTIME	Later Tonight I'm All A-Twitter Over You I Like It Here Dancing in the Dawn We Always Get Our Girl Wintertime

	SWING FEVER	I Planted a Rose One Girl and Two Boys	ON AN ISLAND WITH YOU	Taking Miss Mary to the Ball If I Were You On an Island with You The Dog Song Buenos Noches Buenos Aires
1944	GREENWICH VILLAGE	Give Me a Band and a Bandana It's All for Art's Sake It Goes to Your Toes		
1946	HOLIDAY IN MEXICO	You, So It's You	1949 THE BRIBE	Situation Wanted
1948	THE KISSING BANDIT	If I Steal a Kiss Senorita Love Is Where You Find It Tomorrow Means Romance What's Wrong with Me? I Like You Dance of Fury Siesta	1952 SINGIN' IN THE RAIN	Make 'em Laugh

Broadway Melody (Metro-Goldwyn-Mayer, 1929).
Collectors Book Store, Hollywood, CA.

Leo Robin

Leo Robin is the second most successful lyricist in motion picture annals. More than one hundred of his film songs were national favorites. Twenty-four of them made "Your Hit Parade" surveys of the nation's ten top tunes, and ten were nominated for Academy Awards. Robin was born in Pennsylvania in 1900 and studied law at the University of Pittsburg. While trying to establish himself as a songwriter, he earned his living as a newspaper reporter, publicity agent, and social worker. He finally broke into show business in 1925 when his work was included in the Broadway production *By the Way*. Seven more stage musicals followed within three years, including the 1927 sucess *Hit the Deck* for which he wrote the words to "Hallelujah!" in collaboration with Clifford Grey. Robin's Broadway experience made him a natural choice when Hollywood discovered its need for popular song writers. He was placed under contract to Paramount Pictures.

One of the first entertainers signed by Paramount to appear in its new sound productions was 41-year-old Maurice Chevalier who had created a sensation on the variety stages of Europe. Leo Robin was assigned to write lyrics for the 1929 release *Innocents of Paris* starring Chevalier. One of the results was "Louise" which became the almost personal property of the celebrated French entertainer. In 1930, Robin worked on *Monte Carlo*, in which Jeanette MacDonald introduced his classic "Beyond the Blue Horizon."

Robin was in at the start of one of the longest acting careers in screen history when Paramount added crooner Bing Crosby to its roster. Crosby made his film debut as a featured player in *The Big Broadcast* in 1932 singing Robin's words to "Please." Two years later, Robin wrote the lyrics for "Love in Bloom" which Crosby introduced in *She Loves Me Not* (1934). The number earned its lyricist an Academy Award nomination for Best Song the first year the award was implemented. Robin provided songs for a total of ten films in which Bing Crosby appeared for Paramount. Another promising newcomer with whom Robin was associated was 5-year-old Shirley Temple, who played supporting roles in the studio's *Little Miss Marker* and *Now and Forever* in 1934.

Although Leo Robin was assigned to as many as a dozen films a year in 1936 and 1937, there was no letup in the quality of his work. During these years he wrote the words for such "Your Hit Parade" favorites as "I Can't Escape from You," "I Don't Want to Make History," "Moonlight and Shadows," "A Rendezvous with a Dream," "Here's Love in Your Eye," "Whispers in the Dark," "Blue Hawaii," "Sweet Is the Word for You," "Blossoms on Broadway," "Ebb Tide," and "What Have You Got That Gets Me?" "Whispers in the Dark" brought him his second bid for the Oscar in 1937. His third nomination was the lucky one, and Leo Robin won the coveted statuette for "Thanks for the Memory" from

The Big Broadcast of 1938. "Whispers in the Dark" and "Thanks for the Memory" were the first two of his songs to make the number one spot on "Your Hit Parade." He ended ten years at Paramount with another Academy Award contender, "Faithful Forever" from the full-length cartoon *Gulliver's Travels* (1939).

Robin's next five years were spent at Twentieth Century-Fox providing lyrics for Betty Grable in *Moon Over Miami* (1940), *Footlight Serenade* (1942), and *Coney Island* (1943); Rita Hayworth in *My Gal Sal* (1942); and Alice Faye in *The Gang's All Here* (1943).

Beginning in 1945, Robin free-lanced for United Artists, Warner Brothers, Twentieth Century-Fox, Universal, Paramount, and Metro-Goldwyn-Mayer. As long as screen musicals remained in vogue, Robin remained in demand. He received six more Oscar nominations for "So-o-o-o-o in Love" from *Wonder Man* (1945), "A Gal in Calico" from *The Time, the Place, and the Girl* (1946), "For Every Man There's a Woman" from *Casbah* (1948), "This Is the Moment" from *That Lady in Ermine* (1948), "Zing a Little Zong" from *Just for You* (1952), and "My Flaming Heart" from *Small Town Girl* (1953). Two years after his last nomination, Leo Robin retired from motion picture activity. He is now 79.

The Films Songs of Leo Robin

1929	INNOCENTS OF PARIS	Louise
		Wait Till You See Ma Cherie
		It's a Habit of Mine
		On Top of the World Alone
	SYNCOPATION	Jericho
	DANCE OF LIFE	True Blue Lou
		The Flippity Flop
		Ladies of the Dance
		Cuddlesome Baby
		King of Jazzmania
	POINTED HEELS	I Have to Have You
	WILD PARTY	My Wild Party Girl
	FASHIONS IN LOVE	Delphine
		I Still Believe in You
	THE KIBITZER	Just Wait and See Sweetheart
	THE MAN I LOVE	Celia
	CLOSE HARMONY	I'm All A-Twitter
		I Want to Go Places and Do Things
	RIVER OF ROMANCE	My Lady Love
	WHY BRING THAT UP?	Do I Know What I'm Doing While I'm in Love?
		Shoo Shoo Boogie Boo
1930	PARAMOUNT ON PARADE	All I Want Is Just One
		Come Back to Sorrento
	MONTE CARLO	Beyond the Blue Horizon
		Give Me a Moment Please
		Always in All Ways
		She'll Love Me and Like It
		Day of Days
		Trimmin' the Women
		Whatever It Is, It's Grand
	PLAYBOY OF PARIS	My Ideal
		It's a Great Life If You Don't Weaken
		In the Heart of Old Paree
		Yvonne's Song
	VAGABOND KING	If I Were King
		King Louie
		Mary, Queen of Heaven
	DANGEROUS NAN McGREW	Aw C'mon (Whatta Ya Got to Lose?)
	DERELICT	Over the Sea of Dreams
	DANGEROUS PARADISE	Smiling Skies

	MOROCCO	Give Me the Man
		What Am I Bid?
	DEVIL'S HOLIDAY	You Are a Song
1931	MONKEY BUSINESS	Blue Blazes
	DUDE RANCH	Consolation
1932	THE BIG BROADCAST	Please
		Here Lies Love
	ONE HOUR WITH YOU	(I'd Love to Spend) One Hour with You
		We Will Always Be Sweethearts
		Oh, That Mitzi
		What Would You Do?
		Three Times a Day
	BLONDE VENUS	Hot Voodoo
		You Little So-and-So
	TROUBLE IN PARADISE	Trouble in Paradise
		Colet and Company
1933	A BEDTIME STORY	In the Park in Paree
		Look What I've Got
		Monsieur Baby
		Home Made Heaven
	TORCH SINGER	Give Me Liberty or Give Me Love
		Don't Be a Cry Baby
		It's a Long Dark Night
		The Torch Singer
	MY WEAKNESS	Gather Lip Rouge While You May
		How Do I Look?
		You Can Be Had, So Be Careful
	ALICE IN WONDERLAND	Alice in Wonderland
	INTERNATIONAL HOUSE	Thank Heaven for You
		My Bluebird's Singing the Blues
	THE WAY TO LOVE	I'm a Lover of Paree
		In a One-Room Flat
		It's Oh, It's Ah, It's Wonderful
		There's a Lucky Guy
	CRADLE SONG	Lonely Little Senorita
		Cradle Song
	MIDNIGHT CLUB	In a Midnight Club

	THREE-CORNERED MOON	Three-Cornered Moon
1934	SHE LOVES ME NOT	Love in Bloom
	SHOOT THE WORKS	Take a Lesson from the Lark Do I Love You?
	HERE IS MY HEART	June in January With Every Breath I Take Love Is Just around the Corner You Can't Make a Monkey of the Moon
	LITTLE MISS MARKER	I'm a Black Sheep Who's Blue Low-Down Lullaby Laugh You Son-of-a-Gun
	YOU BELONG TO ME	When He Comes Home to Me
	THE TRUMPET BLOWS	The Red Cape Pancho This Night My Heart Does the Rhumba
	COME ON MARINES	Tequila Hula Holiday Oh Baby Obey
	WHARF ANGEL	Down Home
	KISS AND MAKE UP	Love Divided by Two Corn Beef and Cabbage, I Love You Mirror Song
	WE'RE NOT DRESSING	When the Golden Gate Was Silver
1935	THE BIG BROADCAST OF 1936	Miss Brown to You Why Dream? Double Trouble Through the Doorway of Dreams
	HERE COMES COOKIE	The Vamp of the Pampas
	FOUR HOURS TO KILL	Hate to Talk About Myself Walking the Floor Let's Make a Night of It
	ONE HOUR LATE	Me Without You
	THE CRUSADES	Song of the Crusades
	MILLIONS IN THE AIR	Laughing at the Weather Man A Penny in My Pocket

	RUMBA	I'm Yours for Tonight The Magic of You The Rhythm of the Rumba Your Eyes Have Said If I Knew
1936	RHYTHM ON THE RANGE	I Can't Escape from You The House Jack Built for Jill Drink It Down
	ROSE OF THE RANCHO	If I Should Lose You Thunder over Paradise Little Rose of the Rancho Got a Girl in Californ-i-a There's Gold in Monterey Where Is My Love? The Padre and the Bride
	PALM SPRINGS	The Hills of Old Wyomin' I Don't Want to Make History Palm Springs Dreaming Out Loud
	THE JUNGLE PRINCESS	Moonlight and Shadows
	POPPY	A Rendezvous with a Dream
	THE BIG BROADCAST OF 1937	You Came to My Rescue Here's Love in Your Eye La Bomba Talkin' through My Heart Vote for Mr. Rhythm Night in Manhattan
	THREE CHEERS FOR LOVE	Where Is My Heart? Long Ago and Far Away Swing Tap Tap Your Feet
	ANYTHING GOES	My Heart and I Sailor Beware Shanghai-De-Ho Am I Awake? Hopelessly in Love
	COLLEGE HOLIDAY	I Adore You A Rhyme for Love So What!
	THE MOON'S OUR HOME	The Moon's Our Home
	PREVIEW MURDER MYSTERY	Promise with a Kiss
	DESIRE	Desire Awake in a Dream
	IT'S A GREAT LIFE	I Lost My Heart Lazy Bones Gotta Job Now
1937	ARTISTS AND MODELS	Whispers in the Dark

31

WAIKIKI WEDDING	Blue Hawaii	
	Sweet Is the Word for You	
	In a Little Hula Heaven	
	Okolehao	
BLOSSOMS ON BROADWAY	Blossoms on Broadway	
EBB TIDE	Ebb Tide	
	I Know What Aloha Means	
EASY LIVING	Easy Living	
SWING HIGH, SWING LOW	Then It Isn't Love	
SOULS AT SEA	Susie Sapple	
ANGEL	Angel	
CHAMPAGNE WALTZ	Blue Danube Waltz	
	Could I Be in Love?	
	When Is a Kiss Not a Kiss?	
HIDEAWAY GIRL	What Is Love?	
MAKE WAY FOR TOMORROW	Make Way for Tomorrow	

1938 THE BIG BROADCAST OF 1938 — Thanks for the Memory / You Took the Words Right Out of My Heart / Mama, That Moon Is Here Again / Don't Tell a Secret to a Rose / This Little Ripple Had Rhythm / The Waltz Lives On

ARTISTS AND MODELS ABROAD — What Have You Got That Gets Me? / You're Lovely Madame / Do the Buckaroo

GIVE ME A SAILOR — What Goes on Here in My Heart / A Little Kiss at Twilight / It Don't Make Sense / The U.S.A. and You

THE TEXANS — Silver on the Sage

TROPIC HOLIDAY — Havin' Myself a Time

ROMANCE IN THE DARK — Tonight We Love

HER JUNGLE LOVE — Coffee and Kisses / Jungle Love

1939 GULLIVER'S TRAVELS — Faithful Forever / Bluebirds in the Moonlight / All's Well / Faithful / Forever / I Hear a Dream / We're All Together Now

PARIS HONEYMOON — I Have Eyes / You're a Sweet Little Headache / The Funny Old Hills / Joobalai / The Maiden by the Brook / Work While You May

ST. LOUIS BLUES — Kinda Lonesome

$1000 A TOUCHDOWN — Love with a Capital "U"

NEVER SAY DIE — The Tra-la-la and Oom-pah-pah

1941 MOON OVER MIAMI — Loveliness and Love / You Started Something / Solitary Seminole / Hurray for Today / Miami / I've Got You All to Myself / Is That Good? / Kindergarten Conga

TALL, DARK AND HANDSOME — Wishful Thinking / Hello, Ma, I Done It Again / I'm Alive and Kickin'

RISE AND SHINE — I'm Making a Play for You / Central Two Two Oh Oh / I Want to Be the Guy / Hail to Bolenciewez / Get Thee Behind Me, Clayton

A YANK IN THE RAF — Another Little Dream Won't Do Us Any Harm / Hi-ya Love

CADET GIRL — My Old Man Was an Army Man / She's a Good Neighbor / I'll Settle for You / It's Happened, It's Over, Let's Forget It / It Won't Be Fun / Uncle Sam Gets Around

1942 MY GAL SAL — Oh, the Pity of It All / Here You Are / On the Gay White Way / Midnight at the Masquerade / Me and My Fella and a Big Umbrella

TALES OF MANHATTAN — Glory Day

	FOOTLIGHT SERENADE	Living High
		I'll Be Marching to a Love Song
		I'm Still Crazy for You
		I Heard the Birdies Sing
		Are You Kiddin' Me?
		Land on Your Feet
		Except with You
1943	WINTERTIME	I'm All A-Twitter over You
		I Like It Here
		Dancing in the Dawn
		We Always Get Our Girl
		Later Tonight
		Wintertime
	CONEY ISLAND	Take It from There
		Beautiful Coney Island
		Miss Lulu from Louisville
		Get the Money
		There's Danger in a Dance
		Old Demon Rum
	RIDING HIGH	Get Your Man
		Whistling in the Light
		You're the Rainbow
		I'm the Secretary to the Sultan
		Injun Gal Heap Hep
		Willie the Wolf of the West
	COLT COMRADES	Tonight We Ride
	THE GANG'S ALL HERE	No Love, No Nothing
		A Journey to a Star
		The Lady in the Tutti-Frutti Hat
		The Polka Dot Polka
		You Discover You're in New York
		Paducah
		Minnie's in the Money
1944	GREENWICH VILLAGE	Give Me a Band and a Bandana
		It's All for Art's Sake
		It Goes to Your Toes
1945	WONDER MAN	So-o-o-o-o in Love
1946	THE TIME, THE PLACE AND THE GIRL	A Gal in Calico
		Oh, but I Do
		A Rainy Night in Rio
		Through a Thousand Dreams
		A Solid Citizen of the Solid South
		I Happened to Walk down First Street
	CENTENNIAL SUMMER	In Love in Vain
		Up with the Lark
		The Right Romance
1947	SOMETHING IN THE WIND	The Turntable Song
		I'm Happy-Go-Lucky and Free
		I Love a Mystery
		It's Only Love
		Something in the Wind
		You Wanna Keep Your Baby Lookin' Right
1948	CASBAH	For Every Man There's a Woman
		It Was Written in the Stars
		What's Good About Goodbye?
		Hooray for Love
		The Monkey Sat in the Cocoanut Tree
	THAT LADY IN ERMINE	This Is the Moment
		The Melody Has to Be Right
		There's Something about Midnight
		The Jester's Song
		Ooh, What I'll Do
		It's Always a Beautiful Day
1951	MEET ME AFTER THE SHOW	It's a Hot Night in Alaska
		Betting on a Man
		Let Go of My Heart
		Meet Me After the Show
		No Talent Joe
		I Feel like Dancing
	TWO TICKETS TO BROADWAY	The Closer You Are
		Are You Just a Beautiful Dream?
		Baby, You'll Never Be Sorry
		Let the Worry Bird Worry for You
		Big Chief Hole-in-the-Ground
		Pelican Falls High
		It Began in Yucatan
		New York
1952	JUST FOR YOU	On the Ten Ten for Ten Ten Tennessee
		Zing a Little Zong
		The Live Oak Tree
		Checkin' My Heart
		I'll Si-Si Ya in Bahia
		The Maiden of Guadalupe
		He's Just Crazy for Me
		A Flight of Fancy
		Call Me Tonight
		Just for You
		The Ol' Spring Fever

| | MACAO | You Kill Me
Talk to Me Tomorrow
Ocean Breeze | LATIN LOVERS | A Little More of Your Amor
I Had to Kiss You
Carlotta, Ya Gotta Be Mine |
| 1953 | SMALL TOWN GIRL | My Flaming Heart
Fine, Fine, Fine
Small Towns Are Smile
  Towns
The Fellow I'd Follow
Take Me to Broadway
The Lullaby of the Lord
My Gaucho
I've Gotta Hear That Beat | 1955 | MY SISTER EILEEN | Give Me a Band and My
  Baby
There's Nothin' Like Love
It's Bigger Than You and
  Me |

Playboy of Paris (Paramount, 1930).
Academy of Motion Picture Arts and Sciences Library,
Beverly Hills, CA.

Sam Coslow

Sam Coslow

Paramount Pictures bought a controlling interest in the New York music publishing firm of Spier and Coslow in 1929, and the services of Sam Coslow were included in the deal. The studio actually acquired two talented songwriters. Coslow was both a composer and a lyricist although he generally worked in collaboration with other songwriters. He was born in New York in 1902 and was still a teenager when his song "Grieving for You" became a success in 1920. During the next nine years, he created such favorites as "I'm Just Wild about Animal Crackers," "Lonely Melody," and "Was It a Dream?"

Among the brightest of Paramount's contract players was redheaded Nancy Carroll who was frequently paired with singer Charles "Buddy" Rogers. Miss Carroll was one of the first performers with whom Sam Coslow worked in Hollywood. Her 1929 film *Dance of Life* featured Coslow's "True Blue Lou." Another star on the Paramount lot was the ill-fated Lillian Roth, who introduced the Coslow classic "Sing You Sinners" in her 1930 vehicle *Honey*. One of the highlights of the all-star revue *Paramount on Parade* was Maurice Chevalier's rendition of "Sweepin' the Clouds Away" with both words and music by Coslow.

Enthused by the reception moviegoers had given its new find Bing Crosby in the 1932 musical *The Big Broadcast*, Paramount starred the ex-band singer in *College Humor* and *Too Much Harmony* the following year. Two of the numbers written by Coslow for the films became Crosby trademarks: "Learn to Croon" and "Thanks." Less successful that year was the studio's

attempt to turn radio star Kate Smith into a screen personality. Miss Smith made her feature-length film debut in *Hello, Everybody* singing Coslow's "Moon Song," but her movie career failed to take flight.

The most famous song Sam Coslow was ever to write was introduced by Danish singer Carl Brisson in the 1934 film version of the Broadway musical *Murder at the Vanities*. The number was "Cocktails for Two," written in conjunction with composer Arthur Johnston. A lesser Coslow hit that same year was "My Old Flame" sung by Mae West in *Belle of the Nineties*. The controversial Miss West also performed numbers by Coslow in *Goin' to Town* (1935), *Klondike Annie* (1936), and *Every Day's a Holiday* (1937). Coslow wrote "(If You Can't Sing It) You'll Have to Swing It," also known as "Mr. Paganini," for Martha Raye to sing in her screen test. The result was so impressive that Paramount included the tour de force in Miss Raye's first film *Rhythm on the Range* (1936). Two of Coslow's film songs made "Your Hit Parade" during the thirties: "In the Middle of a Kiss" from *College Scandal* (1935) and the title song from *True Confession* (1937).

After ten years at Paramount, Sam Coslow provided MGM with the music and lyrics for "I'm in Love with the Honorable Mr. So-and-So" heard in *Society Lawyer* (1939). In 1940, the songwriter went into business with President Franklin Roosevelt's son James. The men founded a firm that manufactured coin-operated machines that showed filmed short subjects called "Soundies." Coslow then branched out into film production and won the 1943 Oscar for his short subject

Heavenly Music. Feature-length films followed with Coslow producing *Out of This World* and *Copacabana* for which he also wrote songs. After working on English stage and screen productions during the mid-fifties, the composer-lyricist devoted himself to publishing trade periodicals serving the financial community. Seventy-five-year-old Sam Coslow's autobiography, *Cocktails for Two*, was published in 1977.

Year	Film	Songs		Film	Songs
1929	DANCE OF LIFE	True Blue Lou The Flippity Flop Ladies of the Dance Cuddlesome Baby King of Jazzmania		TOO MUCH HARMONY	Thanks The Day You Came Along Black Moonlight I Guess It Had to Be That Way Buckin' the Wind Two Aristocrats Cradle Me with a Ha-cha Lullaby
	FAST COMPANY	You Want Lovin' (but I Want Love)			
	WHY BRING THAT UP?	Do I Know What I'm Doing While I'm in Love? Shoo Shoo Boogie Boo		HER BODYGUARD	Where Have I Heard That Melody?
	THE TIME, THE PLACE AND THE GIRL	Jack and Jill		HELLO, EVERYBODY!	Moon Song Twenty Million People Great Open Spaces Queen of Lullaby Land Pickaninnies' Heaven
	THUNDERBOLT	(Sittin' Around) Thinkin' about My Baby			
	RIVER OF ROMANCE	My Lady Love		DISGRACED	Any Place Is Paradise (as Long as You Are There)
1930	VAGABOND KING	If I Were King King Louie Mary, Queen of Heaven		FROM HELL TO HEAVEN	Nova Scotia Moonlight
	HONEY	Sing You Sinners In My Little Hope Chest Let's Be Domestic I Don't Need Atmosphere What Is This Power I Have?	1934	MURDER AT THE VANITIES	Cocktails for Two Live and Love Tonight Ebony Rhapsody Lovely One Where Do They Come From? Marijuana
	PARAMOUNT ON PARADE	Sweepin' the Clouds Away		EIGHT GIRLS IN A BOAT	This Little Piggie Went to Market A Day without You
	RENO	As Long as We're Together		BELLE OF THE NINETIES	My Old Flame Troubled Waters My American Beauty When a St. Louis Woman Comes Down to New Orleans
	SILENT ENEMY	Rain Flower			
1932	THIS IS THE NIGHT	This Is the Night			
	BLONDE VENUS	Hot Voodoo You Little So-and-So			
	LADY AND GENT	Everybody Knows It but You		YOU BELONG TO ME	When He Comes Home to Me The Bad News
1933	COLLEGE HUMOR	Learn to Croon Down the Old Ox Road Moonstruck Alma Mater Colleen of Killarney Boo Boo Boo Play Ball I'm a Bachelor of the Art of Ha-cha-cha		SEARCH FOR BEAUTY	I'm a Seeker of Beauty
				MANY HAPPY RETURNS	Fare-Thee-Well I Don't Wanna Play Boogy Man
				LIMEHOUSE BLUES	Limehouse Nights
				YOU'RE TELLING ME	Sympathizin' with Me
			1935	COLLEGE SCANDAL	In the Middle of a Kiss
				MILLIONS IN THE AIR	Crooner's Lullaby

ALL THE KING'S HORSES	A Little White Gardenia
	Be Careful, Young Lady
	Dancing the Viennese
	A King Can Do No Wrong
	When My Prince Charming
	Comes Along

CORONADO	How Do I Rate with You?
	You Took My Breath Away
	All's Well in Coronado by
	the Sea
	Keep Your Fingers Crossed
	Midsummer Madness
	Down on the Beach at
	Oomph
	Mashed Potatoes
	I've Got Some New Shoes

| REMEMBER LAST NIGHT | Remember Last Night |

| THE GILDED LILY | Something about Romance |

| ONE HOUR LATE | A Little Angel Told Me So |

GOIN' TO TOWN	Now I'm a Lady
	Love Is Love in Any
	Woman's Heart
	He's a Bad Man

OH! DADDY	Now I Understand
	You Bring Out the Savage in
	Me

1936
| RHYTHM ON THE RANGE | (If You Can't Sing It) You'll Have to Swing It |

IT'S LOVE AGAIN	It's Love Again
	Gotta Dance My Way to
	Heaven

| THE TEXAS RANGERS | The Texas Ranger Song |

| KLONDIKE ANNIE | My Medicine Man |

| POPPY | Poppy |

| FATAL LADY | Bal Masque |
| | Je Vous Adore |

| HEART OF THE WEST | My Heart's in the Heart of |
| | the West |

1937
| TRUE CONFESSION | True Confession |

| 100 MEN AND A GIRL | It's Raining Sunbeams |
| | Music in My Dreams |

THIS WAY PLEASE	Is It Love or Infatuation?
	This Way Please
	Delighted to Meet You
	What This Country Needs Is
	Voom Voom

TURN OFF THE MOON	Turn Off the Moon
	Easy on the Eyes
	Little Wooden Soldier
	Jammin'
	That's Southern Hospitality

EVERY DAY'S A HOLIDAY	Every Day's a Holiday
	Fifi
	Flutter by Little Butterfly
	Along the Broadway Trail

MOUNTAIN MUSIC	Good Mornin'
	If I Put My Heart in a Song
	Can't You Hear That
	Mountain Music?
	Thar She Comes
	Hillbilly Wedding Song

THRILL OF A LIFETIME	Thrill of a Lifetime
	Keeno, Screeno and You
	I'll Follow My Baby
	Paris in Swing
	Sweetheart Time

| DOUBLE OR NOTHING | It's On, It's Off |
| | After You |

| SWING HIGH, SWING LOW | Panamania |
| | I Hear a Call to Arms |

| CHAMPAGNE WALTZ | Paradise in Waltz Time |

| HIDEAWAY GIRL | Beethoven, Mendelssohn |
| | and Liszt |

| MAKE WAY FOR TOMORROW | Make Way for Tomorrow |

1938
LOVE ON TOAST	I'd Love to Play a Love
	Scene opposite You
	I Want a New Romance
	My Mistake

| BOOLOO | Beside a Moonlit Stream |
| | Booloo |

| ROMANCE IN THE DARK | Romance in the Dark |

| YOU AND ME | The Right Guy for Me |

1939
SOCIETY LAWYER	I'm in Love with the
	Honorable Mr.
	So-and-So

| ST. LOUIS BLUES | Kinda Lonesome |

1940	DREAMING OUT LOUD	Dreaming Out Loud	1948	SLEEP, MY LOVE	Sleep, My Love
	BRIGHAM YOUNG, FRONTIERSMAN	There's a Happy Hunting Ground	1951	HIS KIND OF WOMAN	Five Little Miles from San Berdoo Kiss and Run
1944	PRACTICALLY YOURS	I Knew It Would Be This Way	1953	AFFAIR WITH A STRANGER	Affair with a Stranger
1945	OUT OF THIS WORLD	I'd Rather Be Me It Takes a Little Bit More All I Do Is Beat That Gol Darn Drum Ghost of Mr. Chopin	1955	ROMANCE IN CANDLELIGHT	My Heart Says Yes
			1956	FIRST LOVE	First Love
1946	SONG OF THE SOUTH	Song of the South			
1947	CARNEGIE HALL	Beware My Heart			
	COPACABANA	Je Vous Aime Stranger Things Have Happened My Heart Was Doing a Bolero Let's Go to Copacabana I Haven't Got a Thing to Sell We've Come to Copa			

Belle of the Nineties (Paramount, 1934).
Academy of Motion Picture Arts and Sciences Library,
Beverly Hills, CA.

Courtesy of Pat McGuire and Marie Rasch

Al Dubin

Al Dubin

During the first decade of sound, three major studios produced a series of films capitalizing on the popularity of their early screen musicals. Metro-Goldwyn-Mayer followed its 1929 success *Broadway Melody* with *Broadway Melody of 1936, Broadway Melody of 1938,* and *Broadway Melody of 1940.* Paramount's sequels to its 1932 hit *The Big Broadcast* were *The Big Broadcast of 1936, The Big Broadcast of 1937,* and *The Big Broadcast of 1938.* The most popular in these series were the Warner Brothers *Gold Diggers* productions which began in 1929 with *Gold Diggers of Broadway* and continued with *Gold Diggers of 1933, Gold Diggers of 1935, Gold Diggers of 1937,* and *Gold Diggers in Paris* (1938). The man responsible for the lyrics for all of the hit songs that emerged from the scores of the five "Gold Diggers" musicals was Al Dubin.

Al Dubin was born in Zurich, Switzerland. His family came to America in 1893 and settled in Philadelphia, Pennsylvania, where his father practiced medicine. Dubin was educated at the Perkiomen Seminary and began writing lyrics while still in his teens. He was 25 years old when his first successful song, "Twas Only an Irishman's Dream," hit the sheet music racks in 1916. During World War I, he sang in an overseas entertainment unit. On his return from Europe, he worked as a bartender while trying to gain a reputation as a lyric writer. In 1921, he placed a song in the Broadway revue *Greenwich Village Follies.* Four years later, he collaborated on the hit "A Cup of Coffee, a Sandwich and You" introduced by Gertrude Lawrence in *Charlot's Revue.* His first professional association with motion pictures came in 1926 when he wrote lyrics for "My Dream of the Big Parade," which was used by MGM to promote its' silent film *The Big Parade* starring John Gilbert. By the time he was conscripted as a full-time lyricist for sound films, he had added two more Broadway productions to his credits, and the 1928 song hits "I Must Be Dreaming," "Half-way to Heaven," and "Memories of France."

Warner Brothers signed Al Dubin to a contract in 1929 and his work on *Gold Diggers of Broadway* produced the hits "Tip Toe Through the Tulips with Me" and "Painting the Clouds with Sunshine." The next year, he supplied the lyrics for the favorite "The Kiss Waltz" introduced in *Dancing Sweeties.* His musical collaborator on his first films was composer Joseph Burke. Their work as a team ended when Harry Warren joined the studio in 1932. Dubin and Warren provided Warners with more than sixty hit songs during the next six years. In 1933 and 1934, *Forty-Second Street, Gold Diggers of 1933, Footlight Parade, Twenty Million Sweethearts,* and *Dames* featured such Dubin classics as "You're Getting to Be a Habit with Me," "The Shadow Waltz," "Honeymoon Hotel," "I'll String Along with You," and "I Only Have Eyes for You." One of the featured players in these films was Dick Powell who had been discovered working as a master of ceremonies and all-around entertainer in a Pittsburgh movie palace. Powell rose to stardom singing such Al Dubin lyrics as "Don't Say Good Night," "The Rose in Her Hair," "Lulu's Back in Town," "Don't Give Up the Ship," and " 'Cause My Baby Says It's So." Dubin also wrote the words for two songs that became permanently associated with Al Jolson—"About a Quarter to Nine" and "She's a Latin from Manhattan," which Jolson performed in *Go into Your Dance*.

Al Dubin won the second Best Song Oscar ever awarded to a lyricist for "Lullaby of Broadway" introduced by Wini Shaw in *Gold Diggers of 1935*. The year of the award, nineteen film songs with lyrics by Dubin were among the nation's favorites. In addition to "Lullaby of Broadway," his songs that occupied the number one spot on "Your Hit Parade," included "I'll Sing You a Thousand Love Songs" (*Cain and Mabel*, 1936), "With Plenty of Money and You" (*Gold Diggers of 1937*), "Remember Me?" (*Mr. Dodd Takes the Air*, 1937), and "September in the Rain" (*Melody for Two*, 1937). "Remember Me?" was also nominated as the Best Song of 1937.

The partnership of Al Dubin and Harry Warren ended after the films *Gold Diggers in Paris* and *Garden of the Moon*. After leaving Warner Brothers, Dubin returned to Broadway where he wrote the scores for two revues in collaboration with composer Jimmy McHugh. In 1939, he added lyrics to Victor Herbert's instrumental composition "Indian Summer," and the result was heard on "Your Hit Parade" for fourteen weeks. During World War II, Dubin worked for producer Sol Lesser on the screen musical *Stage Door Canteen*. The film earned the lyricist his third Academy Award bid for his song "We Mustn't Say Goodbye." Screen musicals were still among the nation's favorite entertainments when 52-year-old Al Dubin died in 1945.

1929	GOLD DIGGERS OF BROADWAY	Tip Toe Through the Tulips with Me
		Painting the Clouds with Sunshine
		In a Kitchenette
		Go to Bed
		And Still They Fall in Love
		What Will I Do without You?
		Song of the Gold Diggers
		Mechanical Man
		Keeping the Wolf from the Door
	IN THE HEADLINES	Love Will Find a Way
	SHOW OF SHOWS	Ping Pongo
		If Your Best Friend Won't Tell You
		Your Love Is All That I Crave
	SALLY	If I'm Dreaming, Don't Wake Me Too Soon
		Sally
		Walking Off Those Balkan Blues
		After Business Hours
		All I Want to Do, Do, Do Is Dance
	EVIDENCE	Little Cavalier
1930	DANCING SWEETIES	The Kiss Waltz
	SHE COULDN'T SAY NO	Watching My Dreams Go By
		Darn Fool Woman like Me
		Bouncing the Baby Around
	HOLD EVERYTHING	Take It on the Chin
		When Little Red Roses Get the Blues for You
		Sing a Little Theme Song
		Physically Fit
		Isn't This a Cock-eyed World?
		Girls We Remember
		All Alone Together
	TOP SPEED	As Long as I Have You and You Have Me
		Looking for the Lovelight in the Dark
		Knock Knees
	THE CUCKOOS	If I Were a Traveling Salesman

1931	OH, SAILOR BEWARE	When Love Comes in the Moonlight
		Leave a Little Smile
		Tell Us Which One Do You Love?
		Highway to Heaven
1932	CROONER	Three's a Crowd
	BLESSED EVENT	How Can You Say No?
1933	FORTY-SECOND STREET	Forty-Second Street
		Shuffle Off to Buffalo
		You're Getting to Be a Habit with Me
		Young and Healthy
	FOOTLIGHT PARADE	Shanghai Lil
		Honeymoon Hotel
	GOLD DIGGERS OF 1933	We're in the Money (Gold Digger's Song)
		I've Got to Sing a Torch Song
		Pettin' in the Park
		The Shadow Waltz
		Remember My Forgotten Man
	ROMAN SCANDALS	No More Love
		Build a Little Home
		Keep Young and Beautiful
		Rome Wasn't Built in a Day
		Put a Tax on Love
1934	MOULIN ROUGE	The Boulevard of Broken Dreams
		Coffee in the Morning, Kisses at Night
		Song of Surrender
	TWENTY MILLION SWEETHEARTS	I'll String Along with You
		Fair and Warmer
		Out for No Good
		What Are Your Intentions?
	DAMES	I Only Have Eyes for You
		The Girl at the Ironing Board
		Dames
	WONDER BAR	Goin' to Heaven on a Mule
		Don't Say Good Night
		Wonder Bar
		Why Do I Dream Those Dreams?
		Vive la France

1935	GOLD DIGGERS OF 1935	Lullaby of Broadway
		The Words Are in My
		  Heart
		I'm Goin' Shoppin' with
		  You

	GO INTO YOUR DANCE	She's a Latin from
		  Manhattan
		About a Quarter to Nine
		The Little Things You Used
		  to Do
		Go into Your Dance
		Mammy, I'll Sing About You
		A Good Old-Fashioned
		  Cocktail (with a Good
		  Old-Fashioned Girl)
		Casino de Paree

	PAGE MISS GLORY	Page Miss Glory
	BROADWAY GONDOLIER	The Rose in Her Hair Lulu's Back in Town Outside of You Lonely Gondolier You Can Be Kissed Flagenheim's Odorless Cheese The Pig and the Cow

	SHIPMATES FOREVER	Don't Give Up the Ship
		I'd Rather Listen to Your
		  Eyes
		I'd Love to Take Orders
		  from You
		All Aboard the Navy
		Do I Love My Teacher?

	STARS OVER BROADWAY	Where Am I? You Let Me Down Broadway Cinderella At Your Service, Madame Over Yonder Moon
	SWEET MUSIC	Sweet Music
	LIVING ON VELVET	Living on Velvet
	IN CALIENTE	Muchacha

1936	CAIN AND MABEL	I'll Sing You a Thousand Love Songs Coney Island Here Comes Chiquita
	GOLD DIGGERS OF 1937	With Plenty of Money and You All's Fair in Love and War

	SING ME A LOVE SONG	Summer Night
		The Little House That Love
		  Built
		That's the Least You Can Do
		  for a Lady

	HEARTS DIVIDED	My Kingdom for a Kiss Two Hearts Divided

	COLLEEN	I Don't Have to Dream
		  Again
		You Gotta Know How to
		  Dance
		An Evening with You
		Boulevardier from the Bronx

	SONS O' GUNS	For a Buck and a Quarter a Day
	STOLEN HOLIDAY	Stolen Holiday
1937	MR. DODD TAKES THE AIR	Remember Me? Am I in Love? If I Were a Little Pond Lily The Girl You Used to Be Here Comes the Sandman

	THE SINGING MARINE	The Song of the Marines
		I Know Now
		'Cause My Baby Says It's So
		The Lady Who Couldn't Be
		  Kissed
		You Can't Run Away from
		  Love Tonight

	MELODY FOR TWO	September in the Rain Melody for Two
	SAN QUENTIN	How Could You?
	MARKED WOMAN	My Silver Dollar Man

1938	GOLD DIGGERS IN PARIS	The Latin Quarter
		A Stranger in Paree
		I Wanna Go Back to Bali

GARDEN OF THE MOON

Garden of the Moon
Confidentially
The Girl Friend of a
  Whirling Dervish
Love Is Where You Find It
The Lady on the Two Cent
  Stamp

1940   THE SANTA FE TRAIL   Along the Santa Fe Trail

1943   STAGE DOOR CANTEEN

We Mustn't Say Goodbye
She's a Bombshell from
  Brooklyn
American Boy
Don't Worry Island
Quick Sands
A Rookie and His Rhythm
Sleep, Baby, Sleep
We'll Meet in the Funniest
  Places
You're Pretty Terrific
  Yourself

Gold Diggers of 1933 (Warner Brothers, 1933).
Academy of Motion Picture Arts and Sciences Library,
Beverly Hills, CA.

Courtesy of Mrs. Richard Whiting

Richard Whiting

Richard Whiting had the shortest film career of any of the great songwriters of Hollywood. Although he wrote for motion pictures over a span of only nine years, more than fifty of his film songs were best sellers.

Whiting was born in Peoria, Illinois, in 1891. After graduating from a Los Angeles military academy, he booked engagements as a singer in vaudeville. When he realized the limitations of his vocal ability, he took a job in the Detroit office of the Remick Music Corporation and began spending his nights playing the piano in a hotel orchestra. Whiting was 22 years old when he began having success as a composer of popular music. His songwriting career received a considerable boost when Al Jolson performed Whiting's "Where the Black-Eyed Susans Grow" in the 1916 Broadway production *Robinson Crusoe, Jr.* Two years later, the composer made the big time with his melody "Till We Meet Again" which sold more than five million copies of sheet music! The next decade brought Whiting credits in four more Playbills, and added the classics "Japanese Sandman," "Ain't We Got Fun?," "Sleepy Time Gal," "Breezin' Along with the Breeze," and "She's Funny That Way" to his catalog of successes. His impressive list of hit songs made offers from Hollywood inevitable.

Richard Whiting accepted a bid from Paramount in 1929. He was assigned to work with lyricist Leo Robin on songs that the studio's new French import Maurice Chevalier sang in his first film *Innocents of Paris.* Whiting's other projects in 1929 included *Sweetie* starring Nancy Carroll, *Pointed Heels* featuring Fay Wray, and *Close Harmony* with Buddy Rogers. One of Maurice Chevalier's co-stars was 22-year-old soprano Jeanette MacDonald, and Whiting supplied the two singers with

the hits "My Ideal" for *Playboy of Paris* (1930), "Beyond the Blue Horizon" for *Monte Carlo* (1930), and the title song for *One Hour with You* (1932), which was adopted by Eddie Cantor as the theme of his weekly radio show.

In 1933, Richard Whiting began two years at Fox providing compositions for *Adorable* starring Janet Gaynor, *My Weakness* in which Hungarian actress Lillian Harvey appeared, *365 Nights in Hollywood* featuring Alice Faye, and *Handy Andy* starring America's best-known wit, Will Rogers. Whiting's most famous song from this period was "On the Good Ship Lollipop" sung by Shirley Temple in the 1934 musical *Bright Eyes.* In 1936, he was nominated for the Best Song Oscar for "When Did You Leave Heaven?" which Tony Martin introduced in *Sing, Baby, Sing.* The number also climbed to the top of "Your Hit Parade."

His eight years spent at Paramount and Fox appeared to be a mere apprenticeship when compared with the success Richard Whiting achieved under a new contract with Warner Brothers. In his first year with the studio, Whiting worked on *Varsity Show, Hollywood Hotel,* and *Ready, Willing and Able.* These three films introduced no less than fourteen of Whiting's hits, including the popular music standard "Too Marvelous for Words." His score for *Hollywood Hotel* featured a number that became the theme song of the entire film industry—"Hooray for Hollywood." Motion pictures lost the talent of the 46-year-old tunesmith when he died at the peak of his career in 1938. One of Richard Whiting's last hits was the aptly titled "I've Got a Heartful of Music" published the year of his death.

The Film Songs of Richard Whiting

1929	INNOCENTS OF PARIS	Louise Wait Till You See Ma Cherie It's a Habit of Mine On Top of the World Alone		LET'S GO NATIVE	It Seems to Be Spring My Mad Moment I've Gotta Yen for You Let's Go Native Don't I Do? Pampa Rose Joe Jazz
	DANCE OF LIFE	True Blue Lou The Flippity Flop Ladies of the Dance Cuddlesome Baby King of Jazzmania		PARAMOUNT ON PARADE	My Marine All I Want Is Just One
	SWEETIE	My Sweeter Than Sweet Alma Mammy Bear Down Pelham I Think You'll Like It Prep Step		DANGEROUS NAN McGREW	Aw C'mon (Whatta Ya Got to Lose?)
				FOLLOW THRU	A Peach of a Pair
	WOLF SONG	Yo Te Amo Means I Love You		DANGEROUS PARADISE	Smiling Skies
			1931	MONKEY BUSINESS	Blue Blazes
	POINTED HEELS	I Have to Have You		DUDE RANCH	Consolation
	WHY BRING THAT UP?	Do I Know What I'm Doing While I'm in Love? Shoo Shoo Boogie Boo	1932	ONE HOUR WITH YOU	(I'd Love to Spend) One Hour with You Three Times a Day What Would You Do?
	WILD PARTY	My Wild Party Girl		RED-HEADED WOMAN	Red-Headed Woman
	THE MAN I LOVE	Celia	1933	ADORABLE	My Heart's Desire Adorable My First Love to Last
	THE KIBITZER	Just Wait and See Sweetheart		MY WEAKNESS	Gather Lip Rouge While You May How Do I Look? You Can Be Had, So Be Careful
	CLOSE HARMONY	I'm All A-Twitter I Want to Go Places and Do Things		I LOVED YOU WEDNESDAY	It's All for the Best
1930	MONTE CARLO	Beyond the Blue Horizon Give Me a Moment Please Always in All Ways She'll Love Me and Like It Day of Days Trimmin' the Women Whatever It Is, It's Grand	1934	BRIGHT EYES	On the Good Ship Lollipop
				BOTTOMS UP	Waitin' at the Gate for Katy
				TRANSATLANTIC MERRY-GO-ROUND	Rock and Roll It Was Sweet of You Oh, Leo (It's Love) Moon over Monte Carlo
	SAFETY IN NUMBERS	My Future Just Passed (I'd Like to Be) A Bee in Your Boudoir Business Girl Do You Play, Madame? The Pick-Up You Appeal to Me		365 NIGHTS IN HOLLYWOOD	My Future Star Yes to You
				HANDY ANDY	Roses in the Rain
	PLAYBOY OF PARIS	My Ideal It's a Great Life If You Don't Weaken In the Heart of Old Paree Yvonne's Song		SHE LEARNED ABOUT SAILORS	Here's the Key to My Heart She Learned about Sailors

	BACHELOR OF ARTS	Phi! Phi! Phi!
		When the Last Year Rolls
		    Around
			1936	SING, BABY, SING	When Did You Leave
					    Heaven?

	CALL IT LUCK	I'll Bet on You A Merry Cheerio Drinking Song		RHYTHM ON THE RANGE	I Can't Escape from You Hang Up My Saddle Rhythm on the Range
1935	THE BIG BROADCAST OF 1936	Miss Brown to You Double Trouble Why Dream? Through the Doorway of Dreams		ANYTHING GOES	Sailor Beware

			1937	VARSITY SHOW	Have You Got Any Castles,
					    Baby?
					Moonlight on the Campus
					We're Working Our Way
					    through College
					You've Got Something
					    There
					Love Is on the Air Tonight
					Old King Cole
					On with the Dance
					When Your College Days
					    Are Gone

	CORONADO	How Do I Rate with You?
		You Took My Breath Away
		All's Well in Coronado by
		    the Sea
		Keep Your Fingers Crossed
		Midsummer Madness
		Down on the Beach at
		    Oomph
		Mashed Potatoes
		I've Got Some New Shoes			

	HERE COMES COOKIE	The Vamp of the Pampas		READY, WILLING AND ABLE	Too Marvelous for Words Sentimental and Melancholy Just a Quiet Evening

	FOUR HOURS TO KILL	Hate to Talk about Myself
		Walking the Floor
		Let's Make a Night of It
				HOLLYWOOD HOTEL	I'm Like a Fish Out of
					    Water
					Hooray for Hollywood
					Silhouetted in the Moonlight
					Can't Teach My Old Heart
					    New Tricks
					Let That Be a Lesson to You
					I've Hitched My Wagon to a
					    Star
					Sing You Son of a Gun

	THE CRUSADES	Song of the Crusades			
			1938	COWBOY FROM BROOKLYN	Ride, Tenderfoot, Ride I'll Dream Tonight I've Got a Heartful of Music

Varsity Show (Warner Brothers, 1937).
Collectors Book Store, Hollywood, CA.

Arthur Freed

The Academy of Motion Picture Arts and Sciences was established in 1927 by such screen pioneers as Louis B. Mayer, Mary Pickford, Cecil B. DeMille, and Douglas Fairbanks. The Academy's first ceremony to honor its members for outstanding contributions to the film industry was a banquet held in the Hollywood Roosevelt Hotel in May of 1929. Paramount's *Wings* was the first photoplay to be selected as the Best Picture of the Year. Despite the tremendous popularity of screen musicals, only nine of them managed to win the Academy's highest honor during the next forty-nine years: *Broadway Melody* (1929), *The Great Ziegfeld* (1936), *Going My Way* (1944), *An American in Paris* (1951), *Gigi* (1958), *West Side Story* (1961), *My Fair Lady* (1964), *The Sound of Music* (1965), and *Oliver* (1968). Two of these outstanding nine musicals were produced by a man who started his career in motion pictures writing the words for popular songs. Arthur Freed was a virtually unknown lyricist when he was hired by Metro-Goldwyn-Mayer in 1929. At the time of his death forty-four years later, he had given the studio such widely acclaimed musicals as *Meet Me in St. Louis, Ziegfeld Follies, Easter Parade, Annie Get Your Gun*, and the two Oscar winners—*An American in Paris* and *Gigi*.

Charleston, South Carolina, was the birthplace of Arthur Freed. After completing high school, he took a job with a music publisher demonstrating and selling the firm's latest songs. While working as a song plugger in Chicago, Freed met Minnie Marx who was shepherding her sons through their travels on the vaudeville circuit. Mrs. Marx hired Freed and put him in the act. His career as a performer was interrupted by service in the army during World War I. When he returned to civilian life, he supported himself by writing special material for floor shows staged in Manhattan cabarets. In 1920, his work came to the attention of a theatrical producer who included a song with words by Freed in the Broadway production *Silks and Satins*. The following year, he collaborated with an unknown composer named Nacio Herb Brown on the song "When Buddha Smiles," which achieved some success. A bigger hit was "I Cried for You" for which Freed wrote the lyrics in 1923. As the decade of the twenties progressed, Freed began staging plays in Southern California. He was 35 years old when MGM hired him as lyric writer.

The composer with whom Arthur Freed was assigned to work was his previous collaborator Nacio Herb Brown. Of all the songwriters entrusted with the scores for early screen musicals, Freed and Brown were the least known, even in the music publishing world. But it took only one film—the 1929 release *Broadway Melody* with "You Were Meant for Me," "The Wedding of the Painted Doll," and "Broadway Melody"—to remedy the situation. Arthur Freed further enhanced his reputation as a lyricist with his 1929 hits "Singin' in the Rain" and "Pagan Love Song." "Should I" and "The Moon Is Low" became popular the following year. From 1933 through 1937, Freed created lyrics for such MGM films as *Blondie of the Follies, Peg o' My Heart*, and *Going Hollywood* starring Marion Davies; *Hold Your Man* and *China Seas* starring Jean Harlow; *Sadie McKee* starring

Joan Crawford; and *San Francisco* starring Jeanette MacDonald. One of his most outstanding scores was for *Broadway Melody of 1936*, which produced three songs that made "Your Hit Parade:" "I've Got a Feelin' You're Foolin'," "Broadway Rhythm," and "You Are My Lucky Star," which became the nation's number one song. Also in "Your Hit Parade's" top spot was Freed's "Alone" from *A Night at the Opera* (1935) in which his former vaudeville partners the Marx Brothers appeared.

After Arthur Freed became a film producer in 1939, he still functioned as a lyricist on occasion. He received an Academy Award nomination for his song "Our Love Affair," which Judy Garland sang in the 1940 production *Strike Up the Band*. Two of MGM's most highly praised musicals of the forties were Freed's productions *Yolanda and the Thief* (1945) and *Ziegfeld Follies* (1946) to which he also contributed songs. The last motion picture to feature the lyrics of Arthur Freed was the 1952 release *Singin' in the Rain*. In addition to the new song "Make 'em Laugh," the film's score included Freed's popular music standards "Singin' in the Rain," "All I Do Is Dream of You," and "You Are My Lucky Star."

Arthur Freed served as president of the Academy of Motion Picture Arts and Sciences from 1963 through 1967. He died six years later at the age of 79.

1929	BROADWAY MELODY	Broadway Melody You Were Meant for Me The Wedding of the Painted Doll The Love Boat Boy Friend Harmony Babies from Melody Lane		PEG O' MY HEART	I'll Remember Only You
				COLLEGE COACH	Meet Me in the Gloaming
	HOLLYWOOD REVUE OF 1929	Singin' in the Rain Tommy Atkins on Parade	1934	SADIE MCKEE	All I Do Is Dream of You Please Make Me Care
	THE PAGAN	Pagan Love Song		STUDENT TOUR	A New Moon Is over My Shoulder From Now On The Carlo Snake Dance By the Taj Mahal Fight 'em
	UNTAMED	Chant of the Jungle			
	MARIANNE	Blondy		HOLLYWOOD PARTY	Hot Chocolate Soldiers
1930	LORD BYRON OF BROADWAY	Should I The Woman in the Shoe A Bundle of Old Love Letters Only Love Is Real		HIDEOUT	The Dream Was So Beautiful
				RIPTIDE	We're Together Again
	MONTANA MOON	The Moon Is Low	1935	BROADWAY MELODY OF 1936	You Are My Lucky Star Broadway Rhythm I've Got a Feelin' You're Foolin' Sing Before Breakfast On a Sunday Afternoon
	THOSE THREE FRENCH GIRLS	You're Simply Delish Six Poor Mortals			
	GOOD NEWS	If You're Not Kissing Me Football		A NIGHT AT THE OPERA	Alone
				CHINA SEAS	China Seas
	A LADY'S MORALS	Oh, Why?	1936	SAN FRANCISCO	Would You?
1932	BLONDIE OF THE FOLLIES	It Was So Beautiful		AFTER THE THIN MAN	Smoke Dreams
				THE DEVIL IS A SISSY	Say "Ah!"
1933	GOING HOLLYWOOD	Temptation We'll Make Hay While the Sun Shines Our Big Love Scene After Sundown Going Hollywood Cinderella's Fella	1937	BROADWAY MELODY OF 1938	Everybody Sing Yours and Mine Sun Showers I'm Feelin' Like a Million Your Broadway and My Broadway Get a Pair of New Shoes Follow in My Footsteps
	THE BARBARIAN	Love Songs of the Nile	1939	BABES IN ARMS	Good Morning
	HOLD YOUR MAN	Hold Your Man		THE ICE FOLLIES OF 1939	Something's Gotta Happen Soon
	STAGE MOTHER	Beautiful Girl I'm Dancing on a Rainbow	1940	STRIKE UP THE BAND	Our Love Affair
				TWO GIRLS ON BROADWAY	My Wonderful One, Let's Dance

1941	LADY BE GOOD	Your Words and My Music	1950	PAGAN LOVE SONG	The Sea of the Moon
					Tahiti
1945	YOLANDA AND THE THIEF	Coffee Time			House of Singing Bamboo
		Yolanda			Singing in the Sun
		This Is a Day for Love			Why Is Love So Crazy?
		Angel			Music on the Water
		Will You Marry Me?			Here in Tahiti We Make Love
		Candlelight			Etiquette
1946	ZIEGFELD FOLLIES	This Heart of Mine	1952	SINGIN' IN THE RAIN	Make 'em Laugh
		There's Beauty Everywhere			

Broadway Melody of 1938 (Metro-Goldwyn-Mayer, 1937).
Bill Chapman Collection

Courtesy of Mrs. Ned Washington

Ned Washington

The offices of Central Casting worked overtime to supply studios with attractive dancers for the myriads of screen musicals produced in 1929. Lyricists Leo Robin and Sam Coslow had the chorines doing "The Flippity Flop." Al Dubin's lyrics sent them tip-toeing through the springtime tulips, and Arthur Freed insisted they sing in the rain. The girls took another dunking that year "Singin' in the Bathtub." The words they sang while sudsing were created by Herbert Magidson and Ned Washington.

Ned Washington was born in Scranton, Pennsylvania, in 1901. He entered show business as a master of ceremonies during the heyday of vaudeville. He wrote special material for many of the acts he introduced and performed the services of a theatrical agent for some of them. Washington was 27 years old when he placed a song in the 1928 edition of *Earl Carroll's Vanities*. The next year, he collaborated on "Singin' in the Bathtub," which swept the country. The song was introduced in Warner Brothers' all-star revue *Show of Shows*. Eight more films followed before his film career went into a temporary eclipse. In 1934, he signed with MGM, and his songs were included in such popular attractions as *Viva Villa* starring Wallace Beery, *Girl from Missouri* starring Jean Harlow, and *A Night at the Opera* in which the Marx Brothers returned to the screen without Zeppo.

Washington worked at every major studio in Hollywood. He supplied Republic with "Sweet Heartache" for the first film in its "Hit Parade" series. At Paramount, he collaborated with composer Hoagy Carmichael on "The Nearness of You" featured in *Romance in the Dark* (1938). The number was the first of Washington's inventions to be heard on "Your Hit Parade." The Walt Disney Studio was preparing its follow-up to the phenomenally successful *Snow White and the Seven Dwarfs* and engaged Washington to provide the lyrics for composer Leigh Harline's melodies. The score for *Pinocchio* brought Washington two Oscars—one for "When You Wish upon a Star," which the Academy selected as the year's Best Song, and another for the Best Original Score. He also worked for Disney on *Dumbo* (1941) and *Saludos Amigos* (1942). Both films netted him Academy nominations for "Baby Mine" and "Saludos Amigos." He was in the running for the golden statuette again for "Rio de Janeiro" from *Brazil* (1944) and the title song "My Foolish Heart" (1949) which became the number one song on "Your Hit Parade."

The producers of the western *High Noon* were dissatisfied with the rough cut of the film and commissioned composer Dimitri Tiomkin and Ned Washington to write a song to be added to the picture. It was one of the first times that song lyrics were used recurrently throughout a motion picture to highlight its action. "High Noon (Do Not Forsake Me)" earned the lyricist his third Academy Award in 1952. The following year, he was involved in another attempt to accustom audiences to three dimensional films—the Columbia release *Miss Sadie Thompson*. Film patrons were equipped with special glasses to watch Jose Ferrer torment Rita Hayworth. The picture was unsuccessful despite an excellent score that included Washington's seventh Oscar contender—"Sadie Thompson's Song (Blue Pacific Blues)."

Miss Sadie Thompson and *Let's Do It Again* were the last full-scale musicals on which Washington worked.

The balance of his career was spent primarily in writing title songs for dramas and westerns. He received additional Academy Award bids for his lyrics to "The High and the Mighty" (1954), "Wild Is the Wind" (1957), "Strange Are the Ways of Love" (1959), and "Town without Pity" (1961). Ned Washington died in 1976 at the age of 75.

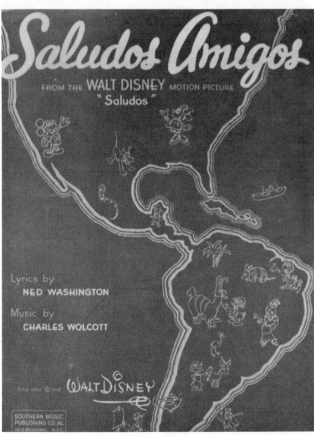

1929	SHOW OF SHOWS	Singin' in the Bathtub
	FORWARD PASS	H'lo, Baby
	TIGER ROSE	The Day You Fall in Love
1930	COLLEGE LOVERS	Up and at 'em
		One Minute of Heaven
	LILLIES OF THE FIELD	I'd Like to Be a Gypsy
	NO, NO NANETTE	Dance of the Wooden Shoes
	LITTLE JOHNNY JONES	Go Find Somebody to Love
		My Paradise
		She Was Kicked on the Head by a Butterfly
1931	ROAD TO SINGAPORE	Hand in Hand
	BRIGHT LIGHTS	Song of the Congo
1934	VIVA VILLA!	La Cucaracha
	GIRL FROM MISSOURI	Moonlight Waltz
1935	HERE COMES THE BAND	Headin' Home
		You're My Thrill
	A NIGHT AT THE OPERA	Cosi Cosa
	KIND LADY	The Duchess Has a Twinkle in Her Eye
	THE PERFECT GENTLEMAN	There's Something in a Big Parade
		Tillie, the Tight Rope Walker
1937	THE HIT PARADE	Sweet Heartache
	THE BIG SHOW	The Lady Known as Lulu
	DODGE CITY TRAIL	Strike While the Iron Is Hot
		Pancho's Widow
		Lonesome River
		Out in the Cow Country
1938	ROMANCE IN THE DARK	The Nearness of You
		Blue Dawn
	TROPIC HOLIDAY	The Lamp on the Corner
		Tonight Will Live
		My First Love
		On a Tropic Night
1939	ALL WOMEN HAVE SECRETS	I Live Again Because I'm in Love Again
1940	PINOCCHIO	When You Wish Upon a Star
		Jiminy Cricket
		Give a Little Whistle
		I've Got No Strings
		Turn on the Old Music Box
		Little Wooden Head
		Three Cheers for Anything
		Hi-Diddle-Dee-Dee (An Actor's Life for Me)
		As I Was Say'n' to the Duchess
	A NIGHT AT EARL CARROLL'S	One Look at You
	ARISE MY LOVE	Arise My Love
1941	DUMBO	Baby Mine
		When I See an Elephant Fly
		Look Out for Mister Stork
		Pink Elephants on Parade
		Song of the Roustabouts
		Casey Junior
	I WANTED WINGS	Born to Love
1942	SALUDOS AMIGOS	Saludos Amigos
1943	FOR WHOM THE BELL TOLLS	A Love like This
	HANDS ACROSS THE BORDER	Hands Across the Border
		Dreaming to Music
		The Girl with the High Button Shoes
		When Your Heart's on Easy Street
		Hey, Hey
	SLEEPY LAGOON	If You Are There
		You're the Fondest Thing I Am Of
		I'm Not Myself Anymore
1944	BRAZIL	Rio de Janeiro
	PASSAGE TO MARSEILLES	Some Day I'll Meet You Again
	THE COWBOY AND THE SENORITA	Enchilada Man
		The Cowboy and the Senorita
		What'll I Use for Money?
	CALL OF THE SOUTH SEAS	Blue Island

1945	MEXICANA	Time Out for Dreaming
		De Corazon a Corazon
		Children's Song
		Mexicana
		Lupita
		See Mexico
		Heartless
		Somewhere There's a Rainbow
1947	GREEN DOLPHIN STREET	On Green Dolphin Street
	I WALK ALONE	Don't Call It Love
	THE LONG NIGHT	The Long Night
1949	MY FOOLISH HEART	My Foolish Heart
	DEADLY IS THE FEMALE	Mad about You
	THE LUCKY STIFF	Loveliness
	MRS. MIKE	Kathy
		Ben-Hur Drip
		Tall in the Saddle
1951	THE WILD BLUE YONDER	The Heavy Bomber Song
1952	HIGH NOON	High Noon (Do No Forsake Me)
	THE HAPPY TIME	The Happy Time
	THE GREATEST SHOW ON EARTH	Be a Jumping Jack
		The Greatest Show on Earth
1953	MISS SADIE THOMPSON	Hear No Evil See No Evil
		Sadie's Thompson's Song (Blue Pacific Blues)
		The Heat Is On
		A Marine, a Marine, a Marine
	LET'S DO IT AGAIN	Takin' a Slow Burn
		It Was Great While It Lasted
		These Are the Things I Remember
		Let's Do It Again
		Gimme a Man Who Makes Music
		Anyone but You
		The Call of the Wild

	RETURN TO PARADISE	Return to Paradise
	TAKE THE HIGH GROUND	Take the High Ground
	SO BIG	So Big
	BRING YOUR SMILE ALONG	Mama Mia
1954	THE HIGH AND THE MIGHTY	The High and the Mighty
	THE ADVENTURES OF HAJJI BABA	Hajji Baba
1955	A PRIZE OF GOLD	A Prize of Gold
	STRANGE LADY IN TOWN	Strange Lady in Town
	THE MAN FROM LARAMIE	The Man from Laramie
	TIMBERJACK	Timberjack
	WICHITA	Wichita
	LAND OF THE PHARAOHS	Land of the Pharaohs
1956	A CRY IN THE NIGHT	A Cry in the Night
	MIRACLE IN THE RAIN	Miracle in the Rain
	THE MAVERICK QUEEN	The Maverick Queen
	THE LAST FRONTIER	The Last Frontier
	THE EDDY DUCHIN STORY	To Love Again
1957	WILD IS THE WIND	Wild Is the Wind
	FIRE DOWN BELOW	Fire Down Below
	3:10 TO YUMA	3:10 to Yuma
	GUNFIGHT AT THE O.K. CORRAL	Gunfight at the O.K. Corral
	SEARCH FOR PARADISE	Search for Paradise
	PICKUP ALLEY	Anyone for Love
	JEANNE EAGELS	Half of My Heart
	NIGHT PASSAGE	Follow the River
		You Can't Get Far without a Railroad
1958	THE ROOTS OF HEAVEN	The Roots of Heaven

1959	THESE THOUSAND HILLS	These Thousand Hills		THE LAST SUNSET	Pretty Little Girl in the Yellow Dress
	THE YOUNG LAND	Strange Are the Ways of Love	1962	ADVISE AND CONSENT	The Song from Advise and Consent
1960	THE UNFORGIVEN	The Unforgiven	1964	CIRCUS WORLD	A Circus World
	SONG WITHOUT END	Song without End	1965	MAJOR DUNDEE	Major Dundee March
	LET NO MAN WRITE MY EPITAPH	Reach for Tomorrow		SHIP OF FOOLS	Ship of Fools
1961	TOWN WITHOUT PITY	Town without Pity	1968	5 CARD STUD	Five Card Stud
	THE GUNS OF NAVARONE	They Call It Love			

Pinocchio (RKO-Walt Disney, 1940).
Academy of Motion Picture Arts and Sciences Library,
Beverly Hills, CA.

Courtesy of Jimmy McHugh Music

Jimmy McHugh

Jimmy McHugh

Jimmy McHugh is second only to Harry Warren in the number of hit film songs he composed. The five dozen motion pictures on which he worked introduced eighty-six melodies that became favorites. Although five of his compositions were nominated by the Academy of Motion Picture Arts and Sciences for its coveted Oscar, none of them were winners.

McHugh graduated from high school in his home town of Boston, Massachusetts. He played the piano during rehearsals at the Boston Opera House and then took a job as a song plugger in the local office of Irving Berlin's publishing company. After four years with the firm, he moved to New York City where he interested the management of Harlem's Cotton Club in including his songs in its floor shows. He was 30 years old when his melody "When My Sugar Walks down the Street" became a best seller in 1924. Two years later, Metro-Goldwyn-Mayer bought his composition "My Dream of the Big Parade" to use in exploiting its silent film *The Big Parade*. McHugh also commemorated the death of the screen's most celebrated lover that year in his song "There's a New Star in Heaven Tonight—Rudolph Valentino." The composer received his first important Broadway commission when he was hired to write the music for the all-Negro revue *Blackbirds*. The show proved to be the longest running musical of 1928, and its hit song "I Can't Give You Anything but Love" became a popular music standard. In 1930, McHugh composed two more classics introduced in *The International Revue*: "Exactly Like You" and "On the Sunny Side of the Street."

Warner Brothers had used Jimmy McHugh's number "Collegiana" in its 1929 film *The Time, the Place and the Girl*, but it was MGM with whom McHugh signed when he decided to concentrate on writing for the screen. The studio included his melodies in such films as *Love in the Rough* (1930), *The Cuban Love Song* (1931), *Meet the Baron* (1932), *Dancing Lady* (1933), and *Fugitive Lovers* (1934). When his contract expired, McHugh free-lanced, working at almost every major studio on the West Coast. He collaborated with lyricist Dorothy Fields and composer Jerome Kern on two songs for RKO's screen adaptation of *Roberta*: "Lovely to Look At" and "I Won't Dance." Both numbers made "Your Hit Parade" and "Lovely to Look At" was nominated as the Best Song of 1935. McHugh created "I'm in the Mood for Love" for Paramount's *Every Night at Eight* (1935), "I'm Shooting High" for Fox's *King of Burlesque* (1935), the title song for RKO's *Let's Sing Again* (1936), and "Where Are You?" and "You're a Sweetheart" for Universal's 1937 releases *Top of the Town* and *You're a Sweetheart*. All these McHugh compositions were on the surveys of America's ten favorite songs. One of the stars with whom the composer was associated was Deanna Durbin who introduced his second Oscar-contending song "My Own" in *That Certain Age* (1938). His third chance at the Best Song award came in 1940 when "I'd Know You Anywhere" was among the entries.

The screen musicals to which Jimmy McHugh contributed during World War II included *Seven Days Leave* (1942), *Four Jills in a Jeep* (1944), and *Something for the Boys* (1944). His work for *Hers to Hold* and *Higher and Higher* brought additional bids from the Academy for his melodies "Say a Pray'r for the Boys Over There" and "I Couldn't Sleep a Wink Last Night." McHugh raised $28,000,000 during a bond rally in Beverly Hills in 1945 and received a presidential citation for his outstanding war efforts. His success as a motion picture songwriter continued throughout the forties and fifties with such compositions as "Life Can Be Beautiful" from *Smash-Up* (1947), "It's a Most Unusual Day" from *A Date with Judy* (1948), and "Warm and Willing" from *A Private's Affair* (1959).

In 1951, McHugh performed his songs at a Command Performance before Queen Elizabeth and the Duke of Edinburgh. The next two years found him appearing in night clubs throughout the United States with a group of eight "singing starlets" that included Darla Hood who had been featured with Spanky MacFarland in "Our Gang" comedies of the thirties.

Jimmy McHugh ended three decades as one of Hollywood's top composers with a song for the film *Let No Man Write My Epitaph* released in 1960. He died nine years later at the age of 74.

Year	Film	Songs
1929	THE TIME, THE PLACE AND THE GIRL	Collegiana
1930	LOVE IN THE ROUGH	Go Home and Tell Your Mother One More Waltz I'm Learning a Lot from You I'm Doin' That Thing
1931	THE CUBAN LOVE SONG	Cuban Love Song Tramps at Sea
	FLYING HIGH	I'll Make a Happy Landing We'll Dance until the Dawn
1932	MEET THE BARON	Clean as a Whistle
1933	DANCING LADY	My Dancing Lady
	THE PRIZEFIGHTER AND THE LADY	Lucky Fella
1934	FUGITIVE LOVERS	I'm Full of the Devil
1935	ROBERTA	Lovely to Look At I Won't Dance
	EVERY NIGHT AT EIGHT	Every Night at Eight Take It Easy Speaking Confidentially I'm in the Mood for Love It's Great to Be in Love Again I Feel a Song Comin' On
	HOORAY FOR LOVE	Hooray for Love You're an Angel I'm Livin' in a Great Big Way I'm in Love All Over Again Palsy Walsy
	KING OF BURLESQUE	I've Got My Fingers Crossed I'm Shooting High Lovely Lady Spreadin' Rhythm Around Whose Big Baby Are You?
	THE NITWITS	Music in My Heart
1936	DIMPLES	Picture Me without You Hey, What Did the Blue Jay Say? He Was a Dandy Oh, Mister Man Up in the Moon
	BANJO ON MY KNEE	There's Something in the Air Where the Lazy River Goes By With a Banjo on My Knee
	HER MASTER'S VOICE	With All My Heart
	LET'S SING AGAIN	Let's Sing Again
	THE VOICE OF BUGLE ANN	There's a Home in the Mountains
1937	HITTING A NEW HIGH	You're like a Song I Hit a New High This Never Happened Before Let's Give Love Another Chance
	TOP OF THE TOWN	There's No Two Ways about It Where Are You? Blame It on the Rhumba Top of the Town Jamboree That Foolish Feeling Fireman, Fireman, Save My Child Post Office (I've Got to Be Kissed)
	YOU'RE A SWEETHEART	You're a Sweetheart My Fine Feathered Friend Broadway Jamboree Who Killed Maggie? Oh, Oh Oklahoma
	MERRY-GO-ROUND OF 1938	You're My Dish More Power to You I'm in My Glory Six of One, Half Dozen of the Other The Grand Street Comedy Four
	WHEN LOVE IS YOUNG	When Love Is Young Did Anyone Ever Tell You?
	BREEZING HOME	You're in My Heart Again I'm Hittin' the Hot Spots

1938	THAT CERTAIN AGE	My Own
		You're as Pretty as a
		  Picture
		That Certain Age
		Be a Good Scout
		Has Anyone Ever Told You
		  Before?

	MAD ABOUT MUSIC	I Love to Whistle Chapel Bells Serenade to the Stars There Isn't a Day Goes By
	YOUTH TAKES A FLING	For the First Time Heigh-Ho the Merry-O
	DEVIL'S PARTY	Things Are Coming My Way
	RECKLESS LIVING	When the Stars Go to Sleep
	ROAD TO RENO	Ridin' Home I Gave My Heart Away Tonight Is the Night
1939	THE FAMILY NEXT DOOR	It's a Dog's Life
	RIO	Love Opened My Eyes

1940	YOU'LL FIND OUT	I'd Know You Anywhere
		You've Got Me This Way
		I've Got a One Track Mind
		(Ting-a-Ling) The Bad
		  Humor Man
		Like the Fella Once Said
		Don't Think It Ain't Been
		  Charming

	BUCK BENNY RIDES AGAIN	Say It My! My! Drums in the Night My Kind of Country

1941	YOU'RE THE ONE	Strawberry Lane
		You're the One for Me
		Gee, I Wish I'd Listened to
		  My Mother
		I Could Kiss You for That
		The Yogi (Who Lost His
		  Will Power)

1942	SEVEN DAYS' LEAVE	Can't Get Out of This Mood
		I Get the Neck of the
		  Chicken
		A Touch of Texas
		Softhearted
		Please, Won't You Leave
		  My Girl Alone?
		You Speak My Language
		Puerto Rico

1943	HERS TO HOLD	Say a Pray'r for the Boys over There

	HIGHER AND HIGHER	I Couldn't Sleep a Wink
		  Last Night
		The Music Stopped
		A Lovely Way to Spend an
		  Evening
		Higher and Higher
		It's a Most Important Affair
		You're on Your Own
		Minuet in Boogie
		I Saw You First
		Today I'm a Debutante
		Mrs. Whiffen

	HAPPY GO LUCKY	Let's Get Lost Murder, He Says Happy Go Lucky Sing a Tropical Song The Fuddy Duddy Watchmaker

	AROUND THE WORLD	Candlelight and Wine
		Don't Believe Everything
		  You Dream
		They Just Chopped Down
		  the Old Apple Tree
		He's Got a Secret Weapon
		Great News Is in the Making
		A Moke from Shamokin
		Roodle-de-Doo

1944	FOUR JILLS IN A JEEP	How Blue the Night You Send Me How Many Times Do I Have to Tell You? Crazy Me Ohio It's the Old Army Game You Never Miss a Trick Heil Heel Hitler
	SOMETHING FOR THE BOYS	In the Middle of Nowhere I Wish We Didn't Have to Say Goodnight Wouldn't It Be Nice? Eighty Miles outside Atlanta Boom Brachee Samba Boogie

	THE PRINCESS AND THE PIRATE	How Would You Like to Kiss Me in the Moonlight?	1948
A DATE WITH JUDY	It's a Most Unusual Day
IF YOU KNEW SUSIE	Livin' the Life of Love My, How the Time Goes By What Do I Want with Money?

	TWO GIRLS AND A SAILOR	In a Moment of Madness My Mother Told Me

1945	NOB HILL	I Don't Care Who Knows It I Walked In (with My Eyes Wide Open) San Francisco
1951	HIS KIND OF WOMAN	You'll Know
1954	THE LEGIONNAIRE	Montmartre
1958	HOME BEFORE DARK	Home Before Dark

	DOLL FACE	Here Comes Heaven Again Hubba, Hubba, Hubba (Dig Ya Later) Somebody's Walkin' in My Dreams Chico Chico Red Hot and Beautiful
1959	A PRIVATE'S AFFAIR	Warm and Willing 36-26-36 Same Old Army
	JACK THE RIPPER	Jack the Ripper

	BRING ON THE GIRLS	Bring on the Girls Uncle Sammy Hit Miami How Would You Like to Take My Picture? You Moved Right In It Could Happen to Me True to the Navy I'm Gonna Hate Myself in the Morning
1960	WHERE THE HOT WIND BLOWS!	Where the Hot Wind Blows!
	LET NO MAN WRITE MY EPITAPH	Reach for Tomorrow

1946	DO YOU LOVE ME?	I Didn't Mean a Word I Said

1947	SMASH-UP	Life Can Be Beautiful I Miss That Feeling Hush-a-Bye Island

	CALENDAR GIRL	I'm Telling You Now Lovely Night to Go Dancing Calendar Girl At the Fireman's Ball A Bluebird Is Singing to Me New York's a Nice Place to Visit Let's Have Some Pretzels and Beer

	HIT PARADE OF 1947	I Guess I'll Have That Dream Right Away I Threw a Kiss to a Star Chiquita from Santa Anita Is There Anyone Here from Texas? Couldn't Be More in Love The Customer Is Always Wrong The Cats Are Going to the Dogs

King of Burlesque (Fox, 1935).
Roy Bishop Collection.

Sammy Fain

Sammy Fain

Sammy Fain joined the cadre of Hollywood songwriters in 1930. Fain was raised on a farm in New York State, and left home after completing high school. It took five years for him to persuade New York publishers that his music was a good investment. One of them took a chance on Fain's melody "Nobody Knows What a Red-headed Mamma Can Do," which made a modest profit. The number was popularized in 1925—the same year Fain had compositions included in the Broadway productions *Sky High* and *Chauve Souris*. The composer finally established himself as a major Tin Pan Alley talent in 1927 when "Let a Smile Be Your Umbrella" swept the country. Three years later, he embarked on a screen career that was to bring him two Best Song Oscars and nominations for eight more.

Sammy Fain worked briefly for Paramount in 1930. His early assignments included *Dangerous Nan McGrew* featuring Helen Kane, *Laughter* starring Nancy Carroll, and *Young Man of Manhattan* in which eighteen-year-old Ginger Rogers made her screen debut. His biggest hit for the studio proved to be "You Brought a New Kind of Love to Me" introduced by Maurice Chevalier in *The Big Pond*. Fain's efforts at Paramount landed him a contract with Warner Brothers, where he spent the next five years. Despite the talent Fain demonstrated with such popular melodies as "By a Waterfall" from *Footlight Parade* (1933), "Lonely Lane" from *College Coach* (1933), "Spin a Little Web of Dreams" from *Fashions of 1934*, and "Ev'ry Day" from *Sweet Music* (1935), the studio entrusted the scores for its most extravagant productions only to composer Harry Warren. Before leaving Hollywood to work on more challenging projects for the Broadway stage, Fain composed the first of his songs that climbed to the top of "Your Hit Parade," "That Old Feeling" introduced in United Artists' *Vogues of 1938*. The number was nominated as the Best Song of 1937.

Sammy Fain created the scores for six Broadway musicals from 1938 through 1941—scores that featured such popular music classics as "I Can Dream, Can't I?," "I'll Be Seeing You," and "Something I Dreamed Last Night." Metro-Goldwyn-Mayer brought Fain back to the West Coast during World War II. He provided the studio with songs for such box office successes as *Presenting Lily Mars* (1943) starring Judy Garland; *Two Girls and a Sailor* (1944) starring June Allyson, Gloria DeHaven, and Van Johnson; *Weekend at the Waldorf* (1945) starring Lana Turner; and *Holiday in Mexico* (1946) starring Jane Powell.

Fain reached his zenith as a motion picture composer after the war. He received his second Academy Award nomination for "Secret Love" introduced by Doris Day in Warner Brothers' 1953 musical *Calamity Jane*. The song was a winner and Fain took home his first golden statuette. His third Oscar contender—the title song for Twentieth Century-Fox's dramatic film *Love Is a Many-Splendored Thing*—also outdistanced the competition and was selected as the Best Song of 1955. Fain then received three nominations in two years when "April Love" was in the 1957 Oscar derby and both "A Very Precious Love" and "A Certain Smile" vied for the award in 1958. "Love Is a Many-Splendored Thing" and

"April Love" each made the number one spot on "Your Hit Parade."

While fulfilling his Hollywood contracts, Sammy Fain composed the scores for eleven more stage productions from 1946 through 1964. His melodies have continued to be regular entries in the Academy Award sweepstakes with bids for "Tender Is the Night" (1962), "Strange Are the Ways of Love" (1972), "A World That Never Was" (1976), and "Someone's Waiting for You" (1977). At the age of 76, Sammy Fain is still in demand in the film industry. In 1978, he wrote both words and music for "Katie" featured in the George Burns vehicle *Just You and Me, Kid*.

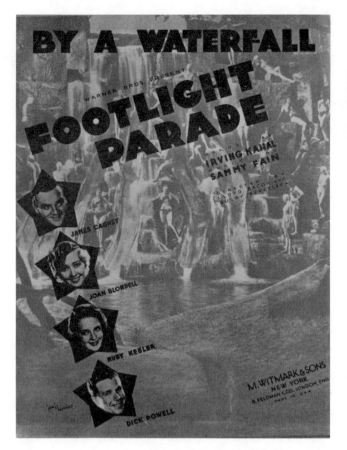

The Film Songs of Sammy Fain

1930	THE BIG POND	You Brought a New Kind of Love to Me
		Mia Cara (My Dear)
	DANGEROUS NAN McGREW	Once a Gypsy Told Me
	FOLLOW THE LEADER	Satan's Holiday
	LAUGHTER	Little Did I Know
	YOUNG MAN OF MANHATTAN	I've Got It
		I'd Fall in Love All Over Again
		I'll Bob Up with the Bob-O-Link
1932	CROONER	Now You've Got Me Worryin' for You
		Banking on the Weather
1933	FOOTLIGHT PARADE	By a Waterfall
		Ah, the Moon Is Here
		Sittin' on a Backyard Fence
	COLLEGE COACH	Lonely Lane
		Men of Calvert
	MOONLIGHT AND PRETZELS	There's a Little Bit of You in Every Love Song
1934	HAROLD TEEN	How Do I Know It's Sunday?
		Simple and Sweet
		Two Little Flies on a Lump of Sugar
		Collegiate Wedding
	FASHIONS OF 1934	Spin a Little Web of Dreams
	EASY TO LOVE	Easy to Love
	MANDALAY	When Tomorrow Comes
	DAMES	When You Were a Smile on Your Mother's Lips and a Twinkle in Your Daddy's Eye
	HAPPINESS AHEAD	Beauty Must Be Loved
	STRICTLY DYNAMITE	Money in My Clothes
	DESIRABLE	Desirable
	HERE COMES THE NAVY	Hey, Sailor!

1935	SWEET MUSIC	Good Green Acres of Home
		Ev'ry Day
		Don't Go on a Diet
		Winter Overnight
		There's a Diff'rent You in Your Heart
		Seltzer Theme Song
	GOIN' TO TOWN	Now I'm a Lady
		Love Is Love in Any Woman's Heart
		He's a Bad Man
	G-MEN	You Bother Me an Awful Lot
1937	VOGUES OF 1938	That Old Feeling
	NEW FACES OF 1937	Love Is Never Out of Season
		Our Penthouse on Third Avenue
		It Goes to Your Feet
		Take the World Off Your Shoulders
		If I Didn't Have You
		It's the Doctor's Orders
1943	I DOOD IT	So Long, Sarah Jane
	PRESENTING LILY MARS	Paging Mr. Greenback
	SWING FEVER	Mississippi Dream Boat
		You're So Different
1944	TWO GIRLS AND A SAILOR	You Dear
	LOST IN A HAREM	Sons of the Desert
	MEET THE PEOPLE	In Times like These
		Schickelgruber
	MAISIE GOES TO RENO	Panhandle Pete
		This Little Bond Went to Battle
1945	THRILL OF A ROMANCE	Please Don't Say No
	WEEKEND AT THE WALDORF	And There You Are
	ANCHORS AWEIGH	The Worry Song
	GEORGE WHITE'S SCANDALS	How'd You Get Out of My Dreams?
		I Wake Up in the Morning
		I Want to Be a Drummer
		Who Killed Vaudeville?
1946	NO LEAVE, NO LOVE	All the Time
		Old Sad Eyes

	HOLIDAY IN MEXICO	These Patient Years Holiday in Mexico
	TWO SISTERS FROM BOSTON	G'wan Home, Your Mudder's Callin' There Are Two Sides to Every Girl The Fire Chief's Daughter Nellie Martin Down by the Ocean After the Show
	LITTLE MR. JIM	Little Jim
1947	THIS TIME FOR KEEPS	Ten Percent Off 'S No Wonder They Fell in Love
1948	THREE DARING DAUGHTERS	The Dickey Bird Song
1950	THE MILKMAN	It's Bigger Than Both of Us The Early Morning Song
1951	CALL ME MISTER	I Just Can't Do Enough for You—Baby Japanese Girl like 'merican Boy Love Is Back in Business
	ALICE IN WONDERLAND	Alice in Wonderland In a World of My Own I'm Late The Caucus Race The Walrus and the Carpenter All in the Golden Afternoon Very Good Advice March of the Cards
1953	CALAMITY JANE	Secret Love Keep It Under Your Hat A Woman's Touch Higher Than a Hawk The Black Hills of Dakota The Deadwood Stage I've Got a Hive Full of Honey 'Tis Harry I'm Plannin' to Marry I Can Do Without You Just Blew in from the Windy City

	THE JAZZ SINGER	I Hear the Music Now Living the Life I Love Hush-a-Bye
	3 SAILORS AND A GIRL	Face to Face There Must Be a Reason I Made Myself a Promise The Lately Song My Heart Is a Singing Heart You're but Oh, So Right Show Me a Happy Woman and I'll Show You a Mis'rable Man Home Is Where the Heart Is Kiss Me or I'll Scream
	PETER PAN	Second Star to the Right You Can Fly, You Can Fly, You Can Fly What Made the Red Man Red? Your Mother and Mine The Elegant Captain Hook
1954	LUCKY ME	I Speak to the Stars The Blue Bells of Broadway I Wanna Sing Like an Angel Love You Dearly The Superstition Song Take a Memo to the Moon
	YOUNG AT HEART	There's a Rising Moon
1955	LOVE IS A MANY-SPLENDORED THING	Love Is a Many-Splendored Thing
	AIN'T MISBEHAVIN'	A Little Love Can Go a Long, Long Way
1956	HOLLYWOOD OR BUST	Hollywood or Bust A Day in the Country It Looks Like Love Let's Be Friendly The Wild and Woolly West
	THE REVOLT OF MAMIE STOVER	If You Wanna See Mamie Tonight
1957	APRIL LOVE	April Love Clover in the Meadow Do It Yourself Give Me a Gentle Girl
	MAN ON FIRE	Man on Fire

1958	MARJORIE MORNINGSTAR	A Very Precious Love	1964	THE INCREDIBLE MR. LIMPET	I Wish I Were a Fish Mr. Limpet March Be Careful How You Wish Deep Rapture Hail to Henry Limpet
	A CERTAIN SMILE	A Certain Smile			
	THE GIFT OF LOVE	The Gift of Love			
	MARDI GRAS	I'll Remember Tonight Bourbon Street Blues Mardi Gras March Stonewall Jackson Bigger Than Texas Loyalty A Fiddle, a Rifle, an Ax and a Bible That Man Could Sell Me the Brooklyn Bridge	1965	JOY IN THE MORNING	Joy in the Morning
			1966	MADE IN PARIS	Paris Lullaby
			1968	IF HE HOLLERS, LET HIM GO!	A Man Has to Love Can't Make It with the Same Man Twice
			1972	THE STEPMOTHER	Strange Are the Ways of Love
1959	THE BIG CIRCUS	The Big Circus	1976	HALF A HOUSE	A World That Never Was
	IMITATION OF LIFE	Imitation of Life	1977	THE RESCUERS	Someone's Waiting for You
1962	TENDER IS THE NIGHT	Tender Is the Night	1979	JUST YOU AND ME, KID	Katie

Footlight Parade (Warner Brothers, 1933).
Collectors Book Store, Hollywood, CA.

Courtesy of the Academy of Motion Picture Arts and
Sciences Library, Beverly Hills, CA

Ralph Rainger

Ralph Rainger

Ralph Rainger was another songwriter who entered the music profession by way of vaudeville. Born in New York City in 1902, Rainger studied classical composition at the Damrosch Institute of Musical Arts. His father was a merchant and wanted his son to become an attorney. Rainger dropped his musical studies and worked his way through law school driving trucks, laboring on farms, and selling door-to-door. Unhappy with the legal profession, Rainger returned to music and took jobs as an accompanist for vaudeville performers. He became an accomplished pianist and advanced from vaudeville to Broadway musicals in which he appeared as a duo pianist with Edgar Fairchild. Rainger was 28 years old when he wrote his first hit melody "Moanin' Low" featured in the 1929 revue *The Little Show*. The following year, he left Broadway for a career in motion pictures.

His first year in Hollywood found Ralph Rainger at United Artists where he provided ex-Ziegfeld star Fanny Brice with the torch song "When a Woman Loves a Man," which she performed in *Be Yourself!* (1930). One of the most popular screen musicals that year was Universal's *King of Jazz* featuring Paul Whiteman and His Orchestra. The Whiteman aggregation included a trio called the Rhythm Boys one of whom was Bing Crosby. Crosby soon began making phonograph records as a soloist. His success as a recording and radio artist led to a contract with Paramount. Ralph Rainger wrote the music for the first hit song to emerge from a Crosby film, "Please" introduced in *The Big Broadcast* (1932).

Another screen newcomer with whom Rainger was associated was Mae West who had served time in a New York workhouse for her allegedly indecent performance in the play *Sex*. Rainger wrote both the words and music for "A Guy What Takes His Time," which Mae West performed in the 1933 release *She Done Him Wrong*. Her suggestive performance in the film was largely responsible for reactivation of Hollywood's own censorship board under the direction of Will Hays. Other Paramount luminaries who benefited from the music of Ralph Rainger were Maurice Chevalier, Claudette Colbert, Shirley Temple, Carole Lombard, Martha Raye, and Dorothy Lamour. Although he generally worked with lyricist Leo Robin as his partner, Rainger collaborated with the celebrated poet and short story writer Dorothy Parker on a song featured in *The Big Broadcast of 1936*. The result, "I Wished on the Moon," made "Your Hit Parade." Sixteen more of his melodies were heard on the broadcasts through 1942.

Ralph Rainger's first recognition from the Academy of Motion Picture Arts and Sciences was an Oscar nomination for "Love in Bloom." Comedian Jack Benny kept the melody alive for forty years with his scratchy violin renditions. The song was originally sung by Bing Crosby in *She Loves Me Not* (1934). Crosby introduced a multitude of Rainger's hits in such screen musicals as *Here Is My Heart* (1934), *The Big Broadcast of 1937* (1936), *Rhythm on the Range* (1936), *Waikiki Wedding* (1937), and *Paris Honeymoon* (1939). An entertainer who was to become Crosby's co-star in Paramount's famous series of "Road" pictures attracted his first film fans singing Ralph Rainger's "Thanks for the Memory." Bob Hope introduced the number in *The Big Broadcast of 1938* and it won its composer the Oscar for the Best Song of the Year. "Thanks for the Memory" became Hope's theme song.

Ralph Rainger ended his contract with Paramount with the Academy Award contender "Faithful Forever" written for *Gulliver's Travels* (1939). Rainger joined Twentieth Century-Fox where he provided melodies for the 1941 musicals *Tall, Dark and Handsome* and *Moon over Miami*. Hollywood's circle of songwriters was shocked to read of the death of 41-year-old Ralph Rainger in an airplane crash near Palm Springs in 1942.

1930	BE YOURSELF!	When a Woman Loves a Man	
	QUEEN HIGH	Brother, Just Laugh It off Seems to Me	
	SEA LEGS	This Must Be Illegal	
1931	ALONG CAME YOUTH	I Look at You and a Song Is Born	
1932	THE BIG BROADCAST	Please Here Lies Love	
	THIS IS THE NIGHT	This Is the Night	
	BIG CITY BLUES	I'm in Love with a Tune	
	MILLION DOLLAR LEGS	It's Terrific	
1933	A BEDTIME STORY	In the Park in Paree Look What I've Got Monsieur Baby Home Made Heaven	
	TORCH SINGER	Give Me Liberty or Give Me Love Don't Be a Cry Baby It's a Long, Dark Night The Torch Singer	
	SHE DONE HIM WRONG	A Guy What Takes His Time	
	INTERNATIONAL HOUSE	Thank Heaven for You My Bluebird's Singing the Blues Tea Cup	
	THE WAY TO LOVE	I'm a Lover of Paree In a One-Room Flat It's Oh, It's Ah, It's Wonderful There's a Lucky Guy	
	CRADLE SONG	Lonely Little Senorita Cradle Song	
	MIDNIGHT CLUB	In a Midnight Club	
	THREE-CORNERED MOON	Three-Cornered Moon	
1934	SHE LOVES ME NOT	Love in Bloom	
	SHOOT THE WORKS	Take a Lesson from the Lark Do I Love You?	

	HERE IS MY HEART	June in January With Every Breath I Take You Can't Make a Monkey of the Moon	
	LITTLE MISS MARKER	I'm a Black Sheep Who's Blue Low-Down Lullaby Laugh, You Son-of-a-Gun	
	THE TRUMPET BLOWS	Pancho This Night The Red Cape My Heart Does the Rhumba	
	WE'RE NOT DRESSING	When the Golden Gate Was Silver	
	COME ON MARINES	Tequila Hula Holiday Oh Baby Obey	
	WHARF ANGEL	Down Home	
	KISS AND MAKE UP	Love Divided by Two Corn Beef and Cabbage I Love You Mirror Song	
1935	BIG BROADCAST OF 1936	I Wished on the Moon Miss Brown to You Why Dream? Double Trouble Through the Doorway of Dreams	
	RUMBA	I'm Yours for Tonight The Magic of You The Rhythm of the Rumba Your Eyes Have Said If I Knew	
	FOUR HOURS TO KILL	Hate to Talk about Myself Walking the Floor Let's Make a Night of It	
	MILLIONS IN THE AIR	Laughing at the Weather Man A Penny in My Pocket	
1936	ROSE OF THE RANCHO	If I Should Lose You Thunder over Paradise	

	Little Rose of the Rancho	
	Got a Girl in Californ-i-a	
	There's Gold in Monterey	
	Where Is My Love?	
	The Padre and the Bride	
PALM SPRINGS	The Hills of Old Wyomin'	
	I Don't Want to Make History	
	Palm Springs	
	Dreaming Out Loud	
BIG BROADCAST OF 1937	Here's Love in Your Eye	
	You Came to My Rescue	
	La Bomba	
	Talkin' through My Heart	
	Vote for Mr. Rhythm	
	Night in Manhattan	
THREE CHEERS FOR LOVE	Long Ago and Far Away	
	Where Is My Heart?	
	The Swing Tap	
	Tap Your Feet	
POPPY	A Rendezvous with a Dream	
COLLEGE HOLIDAY	I Adore You	
	A Rhyme for Love	
	So What!	
RHYTHM ON THE RANGE	Drink It Down	
1937 WAIKIKI WEDDING	Sweet Is the Word for You	
	Blue Hawaii	
	In a Little Hula Heaven	
	Okolehao	
	Nani Ona Pua	
BLOSSOMS ON BROADWAY	Blossoms on Broadway	
EBB TIDE	Ebb Tide	
	I Know What Aloha Means	
EASY LIVING	Easy Living	
SWING HIGH, SWING LOW	Then It Isn't Love	
HIDEAWAY GIRL	What Is Love?	
SOULS AT SEA	Susie Sapple	
1938 GIVE ME A SAILOR	What Goes on Here in My Heart	
	A Little Kiss at Twilight	
	The U.S.A. and You	
	It Don't Make Sense	
ARTISTS AND MODELS ABROAD	What Have You Got That Gets Me?	
	You're Lovely Madame	
	Do the Buckaroo	
THE TEXANS	Silver on the Sage	

BIG BROADCAST OF 1938	Thanks for the Memory	
	You Took the Words Right Out of My Heart	
	Mama, That Moon Is Here Again	
	Don't Tell a Secret to a Rose	
	This Little Ripple Had Rhythm	
	The Waltz Lives On	
TROPIC HOLIDAY	Havin' Myself a Time	
ROMANCE IN THE DARK	Tonight We Love	
HER JUNGLE LOVE	Coffee and Kisses	
	Jungle Love	
1939 GULLIVER'S TRAVELS	Faithful Forever	
	Bluebirds in the Moonlight	
	Faithful	
	Forever	
	All's Well	
	We're All Together Now	
	I Hear a Dream	
PARIS HONEYMOON	I Have Eyes	
	You're a Sweet Little Headache	
	The Funny Old Hills	
	Joobalai	
	The Maiden by the Brook	
	Work While You May	
NEVER SAY DIE	The Tra-la-la and Oom-pah-pah	
$1000 A TOUCHDOWN	Love with a Capital "U"	
1941 MOON OVER MIAMI	Loveliness and Love	
	You Started Something	
	Solitary Seminole	
	Hurray for Today	
	Miami	
	I've Got You All to Myself	
	Is That Good?	
	Kindergarten Conga	
TALL, DARK AND HANDSOME	Wishful Thinking	
	Hello, Ma, I Done It Again	
	I'm Alive and Kickin'	

93

	RISE AND SHINE	I'm Making a Play for You Central Two Two Oh Oh I Want to Be the Guy Hail to Bolenciewez Get Thee Behind Me, Clayton	1943

RISE AND SHINE — I'm Making a Play for You / Central Two Two Oh Oh / I Want to Be the Guy / Hail to Bolenciewez / Get Thee Behind Me, Clayton

A YANK IN THE RAF — Another Little Dream Won't Do Us Any Harm / Hi-ya Love

CADET GIRL — My Old Man Was an Army Man / She's a Good Neighbor / I'll Settle for You / It Happened, It's Over, Let's Forget It / It Won't Be Fun / Uncle Sam Gets Around

1942 MY GAL SAL — Here You Are / Oh, the Pity of It All / On the Gay White Way / Midnight at the Masquerade / Me and My Fella and a Big Umbrella

FOOTLIGHT SERENADE — Living High / I'll Be Marching to a Love Song / I'm Still Crazy for You / I Heard the Birdies Sing / Are You Kiddin' Me? / Land on Your Feet / Except with You

TALES OF MANHATTAN — Glory Day

1943 CONEY ISLAND — Take It from There / Beautiful Coney Island / Miss Lulu from Louisville / Get the Money / There's Danger in a Dance / Old Demon Rum

RIDING HIGH — Get Your Man / Whistling in the Light / You're the Rainbow / Injun Gal Heap Hep

COLT COMRADES — Tonight We Ride

My Gal Sal (Twentieth Century-Fox, 1942).
Collectors Book Store, Hollywood, CA.

Courtesy of David Lahm

Dorothy Fields

Dorothy Fields was the most successful woman lyricist in popular music history—the only woman among the great songwriters of Hollywood. Miss Fields was the daughter of vaudeville comedian Lew Fields of the famed team of Weber and Fields. She was born in Allenhurst, New Jersey, in 1905, and started writing verse while still a teenager. She began her professional career writing material for floor shows staged at Harlem's popular cabaret The Cotton Club in 1926. Two years later, she collaborated with composer Jimmy McHugh on the score for the all-Negro revue *Blackbirds* in which one of the most famous songs she was ever to write was performed—"I Can't Give You Anything but Love." In 1930, Dorothy Fields added two more numbers to her list of songs that were to become popular music standards: "On the Sunny Side of the Street" and "Exactly Like You."

Beginning with the 1929 release *The Time, the Place and the Girl*, songs with words by Dorothy Fields were heard regularly on movie screens. Her early film assignments produced such gems as the title song for *The Cuban Love Song* (1931) and "I'm in the Mood for Love" from *Every Night at Eight* (1935) which became the number one song on "Your Hit Parade." It was in 1935 that Fields began working with one of Broadway's most respected composers, Jerome Kern. Kern came to Hollywood to write new melodies for RKO's film version of his musical comedy hit *Roberta*. Fields collaborated with him on "Lovely to Look At," and it brought the new team an Oscar nomination for the year's Best Song. It

also led "Your Hit Parade." Fields and Kern created the score for *I Dream Too Much* (1935) starring soprano Lily Pons, whom RKO had engaged to compete with Columbia's Grace Moore. In 1936, Fields wrote new lyrics to an old melody by Fritz Kreisler, and the result was the hit "Stars in My Eyes," which Grace Moore sang in *The King Steps Out*. The highpoint of Dorothy Fields' first stay in Hollywood was the Academy Award she received for the "Hit Parade" leader "The Way You Look Tonight" introduced in Fred Astaire and Ginger Rogers' 1936 musical *Swing Time*. She was the only woman to receive a Best Song Oscar until 1968.

Dorothy Fields returned to Broadway in 1939, where she functioned as both lyricist and librettist for more than a decade before resuming her career as a motion picture songwriter. In 1950, she signed with Metro-Goldwyn-Mayer to work on *Mr. Imperium* starring Ezio Pinza, *Excuse My Dust* starring Red Skelton, *Texas Carnival* starring Esther Williams, and the remake of *Roberta* titled *Lovely to Look At*. Her last films were *The Hell with Heroes* (1968) and the screen adaptation of her Broadway success *Sweet Charity* in which Shirley MacLaine appeared in 1969. Dorothy Fields suffered a fatal heart attack in 1974 at the age of 68. She had been at the top of her profession for forty-six years.

1929	THE TIME, THE PLACE AND THE GIRL	Collegiana
1930	LOVE IN THE ROUGH	Go Home and Tell Your Mother
		I'm Learning a Lot About You
		I'm Doin' That Thing
		One More Waltz
1931	THE CUBAN LOVE SONG	Cuban Love Song
		Tramps at Sea
	FLYING HIGH	I'll Make a Happy Landing
		We'll Dance Until the Dawn
1932	MEET THE BARON	Clean as a Whistle
1933	DANCING LADY	My Dancing Lady
	THE PRIZEFIGHTER AND THE LADY	Lucky Fella
1934	FUGITIVE LOVERS	I'm Full of the Devil
1935	ROBERTA	Lovely to Look At
		I Won't Dance
	I DREAM TOO MUCH	I Dream Too Much
		Jockey on the Carousel
		I'm the Echo
		I Got Love
	EVERY NIGHT AT EIGHT	Every Night at Eight
		I'm in the Mood for Love
		I Feel a Song Comin' On
		Speaking Confidentially
		Take It Easy
		It's Great to Be in Love Again
	HOORAY FOR LOVE	You're an Angel
		I'm in Love All Over Again
		Hooray for Love
		I'm Livin' in a Great Big Way
		Palsy Walsy
	IN PERSON	Don't Mention Love to Me
		Out of Sight, Out of Mind
		Got a New Lease on Life
	THE NITWITS	Music in My Heart
	ALICE ADAMS	I Can't Waltz Alone

1936	SWING TIME	The Way You Look Tonight
		A Fine Romance
		Pick Yourself Up
		Never Gonna Dance
		Bojangles of Harlem
		Waltz in Swingtime
	THE KING STEPS OUT	Stars in My Eyes
		Madly in Love
		Learn How to Lose
		What Shall Remain?
1937	WHEN YOU'RE IN LOVE	Our Song
		The Whistling Song
1938	JOY OF LIVING	You Couldn't Be Cuter
		Just Let Me Look at You
		What's Good about Goodnight?
		A Heavenly Party
1940	ONE NIGHT IN THE TROPICS	Remind Me
		You and Your Kiss
		Farendola
		Simple Philosophy
		Back in My Shell
1951	MR. IMPERIUM	Let Me Look at You
		My Love and My Mule
		Andiamo
	EXCUSE MY DUST	Spring Has Sprung
		Get a Horse
		That's for Children
		Goin' Steady
		Lorelei Brown
		I'd Like to Take You Out Dreaming
		It Couldn't Happen to Two Nicer People
		Where Can I Run From?
	TEXAS CARNIVAL	Whoa, Emma!
		Young Folks Should Get Married
		It's Dynamite
		Carnie's Pitch
1952	LOVELY TO LOOK AT	Opening Night
		Lafayette
		The Most Exciting Night

1953	THE FARMER TAKES A WIFE	Today I Love Everybody With the Sun Warm upon Me On the Erie Canal We're Doin' It for the Natives in Jamaica When I Close My Door	Somethin' Real Special We're in Business Can You Spell Schenectady?
1968	THE HELL WITH HEROES		The Hell with Heroes
1969	SWEET CHARITY		My Personal Property It's a Nice Face

Swing Time (RKO, 1936).
Academy of Motion Picture Arts and Sciences Library,
Beverly Hills, CA.

Harry Warren

Harry Warren

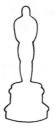

Harry Warren is the most successful composer of popular music in the history of motion pictures. The more than seventy-five films to which he's contributed have introduced 128 songs that achieved popularity. Thirty-six of his film songs made "Your Hit Parade," and 12 of them rose to the number one spot.

Before he began school in his home borough of Brooklyn, New York, his family anglicized his name from Salvatore Guaragna. By the time he was 15, he was playing the drums in a traveling carnival band. He later found employment as a stage hand in vaudeville houses and as a prop man for a New York movie studio. His assignments at the studio increased to doing extra work, playing the piano to help put the silent screen actors in the proper mood, and sometimes performing the chores of an assistant director. After serving in the Navy during World War I, Warren became a pianist in New York cafes and went on the payroll of a music publishing company as a song plugger. He was almost 30 when he wrote his first hit melody "Rose of the Rio Grande" in 1922. It was followed by such successes as "I Love My Baby, My Baby Loves Me," "Away Down South in Heaven," and "Nagasaki."

In 1929, Paramount bought Warren's song "Mi Amado" for Lupe Velez to perform in the talkie *Wolf Song*. Warner Brothers also hired the composer to write new melodies for its 1930 adaptation of the Broadway musical *Spring Is Here*. Warren's score produced the hits "Cryin' for the Carolines" and "Have a Little Faith in Me." Despite their success, Warren remained in New York where he established an enviable reputation as a Broadway composer with such compositions as "Would You Like to Take a Walk?," "Cheerful Little Earful," "I Found a Million Dollar Baby," "Ooh! That Kiss," and "You're My Everything." Warners finally persuaded the tunesmith to join its organization in 1932.

Harry Warren's first year on the West Coast found him creating the score for a musical with a backstage setting. The story concerned the trials and tribulations of assembling a musical comedy. Just before the show's premiere, its star broke her ankle, and an inexperienced chorus girl was trained overnight to replace her. The girl went on and saved the show! The picture was released in 1933 and was a phenomenal success despite the banality of the plot. The elements that saved *Forty-Second Street* from disaster were the elaborate production numbers staged by director Busby Berkeley, the bright performances of newcomers Ruby Keeler and Dick Powell, and the outstanding melodies of Harry Warren, whose score included "Shuffle Off to Buffalo," "Young and Healthy," "Forty-Second Street," and "You're Getting to be a Habit with Me." Anxious to retain the large audiences the film had attracted, Warners rushed two more backstage musicals into release—*Gold Diggers of 1933* and *Footlight Parade*. Both pictures repeated the success of *Forty-Second Street*, and Harry Warren was hailed as one of Hollywood's foremost talents. It was not uncommon for a single Warren musical to produce three or four hit songs. Among his compositions of the thirties that became popular music standards were "Boulevard of Broken Dreams," "I'll String Along with You," "I Only Have Eyes for You," "Remember Me?," and "September in the Rain."

Warren was the second composer to be singled out by the Academy of Motion Picture Arts and Sciences for its Oscar. The winning song was "Lullaby of Broadway" from *Gold Diggers of 1935*. In addition to being selected as the Best Song of the year, it was the first Warren melody to top "Your Hit Parade." Its performance was repeated during the thirties by his "Hit Parade" leaders "With Plenty of Money and You," "I'll Sing You a Thousand Love Songs," "September in the Rain," "You Must Have Been a Beautiful Baby," "Remember Me?," and "Jeepers Creepers." The last two songs brought Warren two more Academy Award nominations.

After assignments on almost three dozen pictures for Warners, the composer moved his piano to Twentieth Century-Fox. The change of scene had no effect on his success. His first year at Fox brought another Oscar nomination for his song "Down Argentina Way." Warren wrote three more Academy Award candidates in as many years: "Chattanooga Choo Choo" from *Sun Valley Serenade* (1941), "I've Got a Gal in Kalamazoo" from *Orchestra Wives* (1942), and "You'll Never Know" from *Hello, Frisco, Hello* (1943). His seventh entry in the Oscar race was another winner, and Warren picked up his second statuette for "You'll Never Know." While working at Fox, Warren provided songs for Betty Grable, Shirley Temple, Sonja Henie, Carmen Miranda, and Alice Faye.

The third studio to benefit from the employment of Harry Warren was Metro-Goldwyn-Mayer, which was known for the excellence of its musicals. Among the best of MGM's productions from 1945 through 1950 were *Yolanda and the Thief* starring Fred Astaire, *The Harvey Girls* starring Judy Garland, *Ziegfeld Follies* starring most of the studio's contract players, *Summer Holiday* starring Mickey Rooney, *The Barkleys of Broadway* starring Ginger Rogers and Fred Astaire, and *Summer Stock* which proved to be the last of Judy Garland's films for MGM. Harry Warren's efforts on these outstanding musicals netted him his third Academy Award for "On the Atchison, Topeka and the Santa Fe" introduced in *The Harvey Girls* (1946).

Harry Warren's last two decades as a motion picture composer have been spent primarily with Paramount, where he created the music for the Oscar candidates "Zing a Little Zong" from *Just for You* (1952) and "That's Amore" from *The Caddy* (1953). The composer received his eleventh bid from the Academy for "An Affair to Remember" (1957). One of the few stars who continued to appear regularly in musicals was Paramount's Jerry Lewis. Warren supplied the scores for the comic's *Rock-a-Bye Baby* (1958), *CinderFella* (1960), and *The Ladies' Man* (1961). Like most of Hollywood's great songwriters when the heyday of the screen musical had passed, Warren's assignments were reduced to an occasional title song, such as "Satan Never Sleeps" (1962) and "Rosie" (1968).

The giant of motion picture songwriters is now 86 years old. He still operates his own music publishing company in Beverly Hills, California.

The Film Songs of Harry Warren

1929	WOLF SONG	Mi Amado
1930	SPRING IS HERE	Cryin' for the Carolines
		Have a Little Faith in Me
1932	CROONER	Three's a Crowd
1933	FORTY-SECOND STREET	You're Getting to Be a Habit with Me
		Forty-Second Street
		Shuffle Off to Buffalo
		Young and Healthy
	GOLD DIGGERS OF 1933	We're in the Money (Gold Digger's Song)
		Pettin' in the Park
		The Shadow Waltz
		Remember My Forgotten Man
		I've Got to Sing a Torch Song
	FOOTLIGHT PARADE	Shanghai Lil
		Honeymoon Hotel
	ROMAN SCANDALS	Keep Young and Beautiful
		No More Love
		Build a Little Home
		Rome Wasn't Built in a Day
		Put a Tax on Love
1934	WONDER BAR	Don't Say Good Night
		Goin' to Heaven on a Mule
		Why Do I Dream Those Dreams?
		Wonder Bar
		Vive la France
		Tango Del Rio
	MOULIN ROUGE	The Boulevard of Broken Dreams
		Song of Surrender
		Coffee in the Morning, Kisses at Night
	TWENTY MILLION SWEETHEARTS	I'll String Along with You
		Fair and Warmer
		Out for No Good
		What Are Your Intentions?
	DAMES	I Only Have Eyes for You
		Dames
		The Girl at the Ironing Board

1935	GOLD DIGGERS OF 1935	Lullaby of Broadway
		The Words Are in My Heart
		I'm Goin' Shoppin' with You
	GO INTO YOUR DANCE	She's a Latin from Manhattan
		About a Quarter to Nine
		The Little Things You Used to Do
		Go into Your Dance
		Mammy, I'll Sing About You
		A Good Old-Fashioned Cocktail (with a Good Old-Fashioned Girl)
		Casino de Paree
	LIVING ON VELVET	Living on Velvet
	BROADWAY GONDOLIER	The Rose in Her Hair
		Lulu's Back in Town
		Outside of You
		Flagenheim's Odorless Cheese
		Lonely Gondolier
		You Can Be Kissed
		The Pig and the Cow
	SHIPMATES FOREVER	Don't Give Up the Ship
		I'd Love to Take Orders from You
		I'd Rather Listen to Your Eyes
		All Aboard the Navy
		Do I Love My Teacher?
	STARS OVER BROADWAY	Where Am I?
		You Let Me Down
		Broadway Cinderella
		At Your Service, Madame
		Over Yonder Moon
	PAGE MISS GLORY	Page Miss Glory
	IN CALIENTE	Muchacha
	SWEET MUSIC	Sweet Music
1936	GOLD DIGGERS OF 1937	With Plenty of Money and You
		All's Fair in Love and War
	CAIN AND MABEL	I'll Sing You a Thousand Love Songs
		Coney Island
		Here Comes Chiquita

SING ME A LOVE SONG	Summer Night	
	The Little House That Love Built	
	That's the Least You Can Do for a Lady	
HEARTS DIVIDED	My Kingdom for a Kiss	
	Two Hearts Divided	
COLLEEN	I Don't Have to Dream Again	
	You Gotta Know How to Dance	
	An Evening with You	
	Boulevardier from the Bronx	
SONS O' GUNS	For a Buck and a Quarter a Day	
STOLEN HOLIDAY	Stolen Holiday	

1937	MR. DODD TAKES THE AIR	Remember Me?
		Am I in Love?
		If I Were a Little Pond Lily
		The Girl You Used to Be
		Here Comes the Sandman
	MELODY FOR TWO	September in the Rain
		Melody for Two
	SAN QUENTIN	How Could You?
	MARKED WOMAN	My Silver Dollar Man
	THE SINGING MARINE	I Know Now
		'Cause My Baby Says It's So
		The Song of the Marines
		Night Over Shanghai
		The Lady Who Couldn't Be Kissed
		You Can't Run Away from Love Tonight

1938	GOING PLACES	Jeepers Creepers
		Say It with a Kiss
		Oh, What a Horse was Charlie
	GOLD DIGGERS IN PARIS	Day Dreaming All Night Long
		The Latin Quarter
		A Stranger in Paree
		I Wanna Go Back to Bali

HARD TO GET	You Must Have Been a Beautiful Baby	
	There's a Sunny Side to Every Situation	
GARDEN OF THE MOON	The Girl Friend of a Whirling Dervish	
	Confidentially	
	Love Is Where You Find It	
	Garden of the Moon	
	The Lady on the Two Cent Stamp	
COWBOY FROM BROOKLYN	Cowboy from Brooklyn	

1939	NAUGHTY BUT NICE	Horray for Spinach
		In a Moment of Weakness
		Corn Pickin'
		I'm Happy about the Whole Thing
	HONOLULU	Honolulu
		This Night Will Be My Souvenir
		The Leader Doesn't Like Music
	WINGS OF THE NAVY	Wings over the Navy

1940	DOWN ARGENTINE WAY	Down Argentina Way
		Two Dreams Met
		Nenita
		Sing to Your Senorita
	TIN PAN ALLEY	You Say the Sweetest Things, Baby
	YOUNG PEOPLE	I Wouldn't Take a Million
		Mason-Dixon Line
		Fifth Avenue
		Young People
		Tra-La-La-La

1941	SUN VALLEY SERENADE	Chattanooga Choo Choo
		I Know Why
		It Happened in Sun Valley
		The Kiss Polka
	THAT NIGHT IN RIO	I Yi Yi Yi Yi
		Chica Chica Boom Chic
		They Met in Rio
		Boa Noite
	WEEKEND IN HAVANA	Tropical Magic
		Weekend in Havana
		Man with the Lollipop Song
		The Nango
		When I Love I Love

	GREAT AMERICAN BROADCAST	I've Got a Bone to Pick with You I Take to You It's All in a Lifetime Long Ago Last Night Where Are You? The Great American Broadcast	
1942	ORCHESTRA WIVES	I've Got a Gal in Kalamazoo Serenade in Blue At Last People Like You and Me That's Sabotage	
	SPRINGTIME IN THE ROCKIES	I Had the Craziest Dream A Poem Set to Music Pan-American Jubilee Run, Little Raindrop, Run	
	ICELAND	There Will Never Be Another You You Can't Say No to a Soldier Let's Bring New Glory to Old Glory I Like a Military Tune	
1943	HELLO, FRISCO, HELLO	You'll Never Know	
	SWEET ROSIE O'GRADY	My Heart Tells Me The Wishing Waltz Get Your Police Gazette My Sam Goin' to the County Fair Where, Oh Where, Oh Where Is the Groom?	
	THE GANG'S ALL HERE	No Love, No Nothing A Journey to a Star The Lady in the Tutti-Fruiti Hat The Polka Dot Polka You Discover You're in New York Paducah Minnie's in the Money	
1944	GREENWICH VILLAGE	I Like to Be Loved by You	
1945	DIAMOND HORSESHOE	The More I See You In Acapulco I Wish I Knew The Mink Lament Play Me an Old-Fashioned Melody A Nickel's Worth of Jive Welcome to the Diamond Horseshoe Cooking Up a Show	

	YOLANDA AND THE THIEF	Coffee Time Yolanda This Is a Day for Love Angel Will You Marry Me? Candlelight	
1946	THE HARVEY GIRLS	On the Atchison, Topeka and the Santa Fe Wait and See The Wild, Wild West In the Valley (Where the Evenin' Sun Goes Down) Swing Your Partner Round and Round It's a Great Big World	
	ZIEGFELD FOLLIES	This Heart of Mine	
1948	SUMMER HOLIDAY	The Stanley Steamer It's Our Home Town Afraid to Fall in Love Dan-Dan-Danville High Independence Day I Think You're the Sweetest Kid I've Ever Known The Weary Blues Never Again	
1949	MY DREAM IS YOURS	My Dream Is Yours Someone like You Love Finds a Way Freddie, Get Ready Ric, Tic, Tic	
	THE BARKLEYS OF BROADWAY	You'd Be Hard to Replace Swing Trot Week-End in the Country Manhattan Downbeat Shoes with Wings On My One and Only Highland Fling	
1950	SUMMER STOCK	Friendly Star If You Feel like Singing, Sing Mem'ry Island Dig-Dig-Dig for Your Dinner Happy Harvest You, Wonderful You	

	PAGAN LOVE SONG	The Sea of the Moon
		Tahiti
		The House of Singing Bamboo
		Singing in the Sun
		Why Is Love So Crazy?
		Music on the Water
		Here in Tahiti We Make Love
		Etiquette
1951	TEXAS CARNIVAL	Whoa, Emma!
		Young Folks Should Get Married
		It's Dynamite
		Carnie's Pitch
1952	JUST FOR YOU	Zing a Little Zong
		Just for You
		I'll Si-Si Ya in Bahia
		A Flight of Fancy
		The Live Oak Tree
		Checkin' My Heart
		The Maiden of Guadalupe
		He's Just Crazy for Me
		Call Me Tonight
		The Ol' Spring Fever
		On the Ten Ten for Ten Ten Tennessee
	THE BELLE OF NEW YORK	When I'm Out with the Belle of New York
		A Bride's Wedding-Day Song
		Baby Doll
		Oops!
		Naughty but Nice
		Seeing's Believing
		Bachelor Dinner Song
		Thank You, Mr. Currier, Thank You, Mr. Ives
		I Wanna Be a Dancin' Man
		I Love to Beat a Big Bass Drum

	SKIRTS AHOY!	The Navy Waltz
		Hilda Matilda
		What Good Is a Guy without a Girl?
		What Makes a Wave?
		I Got a Funny Feeling
		Glad to Have You Aboard
		We Will Fight
		Hold Me Close to You
1953	THE CADDY	That's Amore
		You're the Right One
		The Gay Continental
		It's a Whistle-in' Kinda Mornin'
		One Big Love
		What Wouldcha Do without Me?
1955	ARTISTS AND MODELS	Inamorata
		Artists and Models
		The Bat Lady
		The Lucky Song
		When You Pretend
		You Look So Familiar
	MARTY	Marty
	THE BIRDS AND THE BEES	The Birds and the Bees
		La Parisienne
1956	SPRING REUNION	Spring Reunion
1957	AN AFFAIR TO REMEMBER	An Affair to Remember
		Tomorrowland
		The Tiny Scout
		Contin-u-e
1958	SEPARATE TABLES	Separate Tables
	ROCK-A-BYE BABY	Dormi, Dormi, Dormi
		Rock-a-Bye Baby
		Why Can't He Care for Me?
		Love Is a Lonely Thing
		The White Virgin of the Nile
		The Land of La La La
1959	THESE THOUSAND HILLS	These Thousand Hills

1960	CINDERFELLA	Somebody The Princess Waltz Let Me Be People The Other Fella (A Soliloquy)	1961	THE LADIES' MAN	He Doesn't Know Don't Go to Paris
			1962	SATAN NEVER SLEEPS	Satan Never Sleeps
			1968	ROSIE	Rosie

Go into Your Dance (Warner Brothers, 1935).
Academy of Motion Picture Arts and Sciences Library,
Beverly Hills, CA.

Courtesy of Mrs. Walter Donaldson

Walter Donaldson

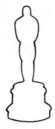

Walter Donaldson had one of the most impressive records of any of the composers in the first wave of popular songwriters conscripted by the moviemakers. More than seventy of the melodies he created before the Hollywood sound panic became national favorites.

Donaldson was born in Brooklyn, New York, in 1893. While in high school, he wrote tunes for shows staged by the students. After he graduated, he was employed in a minor capacity by a brokerage firm on Wall Street. Donaldson left the stock and bond business to accept a position with a music publishing firm. His first composition to attract the attention of Tin Pan Alley was "Just Try to Picture Me Way Down in Tennessee," which went on sale in 1915. When the United States went to war in 1917, he entertained servicemen at Army camps. One of the biggest hit songs to follow the armistice was Donaldson's "How Ya Gonna Keep 'em Down on the Farm?"

During the Roaring Twenties, Donaldson added "My Mammy," "Carolina in the Morning," "My Buddy," "Beside a Babbling Brook," "Yes Sir, That's My Baby," and "After I Say I'm Sorry" to his catalog of popular music standards. His songs helped further the career of the "Queen of the Torch Song," Ruth Etting, who made best-selling recordings of Donaldson's "My Blue Heaven," "At Sundown," and "Sam, the Old Accordian Man." Miss Etting appeared in Florenz Ziegfeld's 1928 musical comedy Whoopee, in which she and Eddie Cantor introduced Donaldson's classics "Love Me or Leave Me" and "Makin' Whoopee." By that time, the composer was operating his own publishing company and occasionally writing lyrics as well as music.

Movie theaters screened the first two films featuring songs by Walter Donaldson in 1928: Warming Up starring Jean Arthur and Richard Dix, and Hit of the Show starring Joe E. Brown. They were followed by Hot for Paris in 1929, and Cameo Kirby and Whoopee in 1930. Whoopee included a hit written by Donaldson especially for the screen adaptation—"My Baby Just Cares for Me." Donaldson signed with Metro-Goldwyn-Mayer in 1933 and spent the rest of his career writing primarily for motion pictures.

Walter Donaldson's first assignment under his new contract was the comedy The Prizefighter and the Lady, in which Myrna Loy appeared with two heavyweight champions, Max Baer and Primo Carnera. In 1934, he provided songs for the dramas Operator 13, starring Marion Davies and Gary Cooper, and Forsaking All Others, starring Joan Crawford and Clark Gable, and the comedy Hollywood Party featuring Jimmy Durante. Also in 1934, Donaldson was loaned to Samuel Goldwyn for the Eddie Cantor musical Kid Millions. His score for Kid Millions produced three hit songs, "An Earful of Music," "Okay, Toots," and "When My Ship Comes In." The tunesmith faced his most challenging film project when he was assigned to an MGM musical concerning the career of Florenz Ziegfeld and his marriages to Anna Held and Billie Burke. The studio spared no expense on the extravaganza. The set for the film's finale consisted of ramps spiraling a huge revolving column and was one of the largest ever constructed on a Hollywood sound stage. The picture's production values could easily have overpowered the score, but Walter Donaldson came up with three melodies that more than held their own against the sets and costumes: "You," "You Never Looked So Beautiful," and "You Gotta Pull Strings." "You" was one of the year's most popular songs rising to the top of "Your Hit Parade." *The Great Ziegfeld*, starring William Powell, Myrna Loy, and Luise Rainer, was selected by the Academy of Motion Picture Arts and Sciences as the Best Picture of 1936.

Donaldson had two of his compositions in the number one spot on "Your Hit Parade" in 1936: "You" and "Did I Remember." "Did I Remember" from *Suzy* earned the composer an Academy Award nomination. Donaldson remained with MGM throughout the 1930s. After leaving the studio, he worked at Universal and Columbia on low-budget musicals, such as *Give Out, Sisters; What's Buzzin', Cousin?;* and *Beautiful but Broke.* Screen musicals were still profitable enterprises when Walter Donaldson died in 1947 at the age of 54.

1928	WARMING UP	Out of the Dawn
	HIT OF THE SHOW	You're in Love and I'm in Love
1929	HOT FOR PARIS	Sweet Nothings of Love
		Duke of Kakiak
		Sing Your Little Folk Song
1930	CAMEO KIRBY	Romance
		After a Million Dreams
	WHOOPEE	My Baby Just Cares for Me
		A Girl Friend of a Boy Friend of Mine
1933	THE PRIZEFIGHTER AND THE LADY	You've Got Everything
1934	OPERATOR 13	Sleepy Head
		Once in a Lifetime
	HOLLYWOOD PARTY	I've Had My Moments
		Feelin' High
	KID MILLIONS	An Earful of Music
		Okay, Toots
		When My Ship Comes In
		Ice Cream Fantasy
	LET'S TALK IT OVER	Long Live Love
	FORSAKING ALL OTHERS	Forsaking All Others
	MILLION DOLLAR RANSOM	You'll Never Know
	GAY BRIDE	Mississippi Honeymoon
1935	HERE COMES THE BAND	Tender Is the Night
	RECKLESS	Cyclone

1936	SUZY	Did I Remember
	THE GREAT ZIEGFELD	You
		You Never Looked So Beautiful
		You Gotta Pull Strings
		Queen of the Jungle
		She's a Follies Girl
	SINNER TAKE ALL	I'd Be Lost without You
	THE OLD SOAK	You've Got a Certain Something
	PICCADILLY JIM	Night of Nights
	AFTER THE THIN MAN	Blow That Horn
	HIS BROTHER'S WIFE	Can't We Fall in Love?
1937	MADAME X	You're Setting Me on Fire
	SARATOGA	The Horse with the Dreamy Eyes
		Saratoga
	MAN OF THE PEOPLE	Let Me Day Dream
1939	THAT'S RIGHT—YOU'RE WRONG	I'm Fit to Be Tied
	BROADWAY SERENADE	Time Changes Everything but Love
1940	TWO GIRLS ON BROADWAY	Rancho Santa Fe
		True Love
		Maybe It's the Moon
1942	PANAMA HATTIE	Did I Get Stinking at the Club Savoy!
	GIVE OUT, SISTERS	The New Generation
1943	WHAT'S BUZZIN' COUSIN?	Nevada
1944	BEAUTIFUL BUT BROKE	Keeping It Private
	FOLLOW THE BOYS	Tonight
1947	BIG TOWN	It's a Small World

The Great Ziegfeld (Metro-Goldwyn-Mayer, 1936).
Academy of Motion Picture Arts and Sciences Library,
Beverly Hills, CA.

Courtesy of Mrs. Gus Kahn

Gus Kahn

Gus Kahn's reputation as a successful popular song writer was second only to that of Irving Berlin at the time the two men began working separately for motion pictures. Although Berlin wrote both words and music, Kahn's talent was limited to lyric writing.

Like Berlin, Kahn was the son of immigrant parents. The Kahns came to the United States from Coblenz, Germany, when their son was 5 years old. They settled in Chicago, where Gus was educated in public schools. He began earning his living as a clerk in a mail order house and broke into the music business writing special material for vaudeville performers. Kahn's first hit song, "My Dreamy China Lady," was published in 1906 when he was only 20. During his early years as a songwriter, his primary collaborator was composer Grace LeBoy, whom he married. The first of Kahn's numbers to become a popular music standard, "Memories," was popularized in 1915. His Broadway career began with the 1916 edition of the revue *The Passing Show*, which featured his "Pretty Baby." During the next thirteen years, eleven more stage productions had songs with lyrics by Gus Kahn, including the classics "Toot, Toot Tootsie," "Carolina in the Morning," "Love Me or Leave Me," "Makin' Whoopee," and "Liza." While engaged on Broadway musicals, Kahn continued to write independent numbers aimed strictly at the sale of sheet music and phonograph records. During the twenties, he was responsible for the words to an average of eight hits a year. Among them were the standouts "Ain't

We Got Fun?," "I'll See You in My Dreams," "Nobody's Sweetheart," "Charley, My Boy," "Yes Sir, That's My Baby," and "Chlo-e."

Although Gus Kahn's lyrics were heard in films as early as the 1928 release *Hit of the Show*, it wasn't until 1933 that he became a full-time motion picture songwriter. That year, he and Edward Eliscu shared the lyric credits on *Flying Down to Rio*. The film was the first to feature Fred Astaire and Ginger Rogers as a team, and its score included "Orchids in the Moonlight," "The Carioca," "Music Makes Me," and the title song. When the Academy of Motion Picture Arts and Sciences announced the nominees for its first Best Song award in 1934, it included Gus Kahn for "The Carioca."

Metropolitan opera soprano Grace Moore had enjoyed a short career at Metro-Goldwyn-Mayer during the early days of sound films. After screen musicals returned to vogue in 1933, Columbia decided to finance Miss Moore's comeback in *One Night of Love*. To the surprise of most Hollywood moguls, movie fans stood in line to hear the star's renditions of operatic arias. The only contemporary number in *One Night of Love* was Gus Kahn's title song, which became a national favorite. Grace Moore's sudden popularity caused other studios to import opera singers, and divas Lily Pons and Gladys Swarthout were soon facing the cameras. Gus Kahn also met success with his title song for Grace Moore's second Columbia film *Love Me Forever* released in 1935. The broadcasts of "Your Hit Parade" began that year, and four of Kahn's film songs made the first surveys of the nation's most popular songs: "Love Me Forever," "Thanks a Million," "I'm Sitting High on a Hilltop," and "You're All I Need," which made the "Hit Parade's" top spot.

The studio for which Gus Kahn worked most frequently was MGM. He provided it with hit songs for *San Francisco* (1936) starring Jeanette MacDonald, *Love on the Run* (1936) starring Joan Crawford, *A Day at the Races* (1937) starring the Marx Brothers, *Maytime* (1937) and *Girl of the Golden West* (1938) starring Jeanette MacDonald and Nelson Eddy, *Honolulu* (1939) starring Eleanor Powell, and *Idiot's Delight* (1939) starring Norma Shearer and Clark Gable. Kahn received his second Academy Award nomination for "Waltzing in the Clouds," which Deanna Durbin introduced in Universal's *Spring Parade* in 1940.

One of the last projects on which Kahn was employed was MGM's *Ziegfeld Girl* (1941). The film's highlight was a spectacular production number in which showgirls paraded to his song "You Stepped Out of a Dream." The sequence represented the screen musical at its best. Fifty-four-year-old Gus Kahn died the year *Ziegfeld Girl* was released. Hollywood paid tribute to one of its greatest songwriters in Kahn's film biography, *I'll See You in My Dreams*, released in 1951.

1928	HIT OF THE SHOW	Waitin' for Katy	GAY BRIDE	Mississippi Honeymoon

1930	WHOOPEE	My Baby Just Cares for Me
		A Girl Friend of a Boy
		  Friend of Mine
			FORSAKING ALL
			  OTHERS
				Forsaking All Others

			LAUGHING BOY	The Call of Love

1931	HOLY TERROR	Do You Believe in Love at
		  First Sight?
			1935 THANKS A MILLION	Thanks a Million
				I'm Sitting High on a
				  Hilltop

1933	FLYING DOWN TO RIO	The Carioca Orchids in the Moonlight Flying Down to Rio Music Makes Me		Sugar Plum New O'leans Sing Brother Sing I've Got a Pocketful of Sunshine
	PEG O' MY HEART	Sweetheart Darlin'		
	THE PRIZEFIGHTER AND THE LADY	You've Got Everything Downstream Drifter	LOVE ME FOREVER	Love Me Forever Whoa!
	THE WHITE SISTER	Drifting on a Blue Lagoon	ESCAPADE	You're All I Need
	STORM AT DAYBREAK	I Will Be a Soldier's Bride Oh, How Weary	THE GIRL FRIEND	Two Together What Is This Power? Welcome to Napoleon Napoleon's Exile
	SAMARANG	Out of the Deep		
1934	ONE NIGHT OF LOVE	One Night of Love	MUTINY ON THE BOUNTY	Love Song of Tahiti
	BOTTOMS UP	Waitin' at the Gate for Katy		
	STINGAREE	Tonight Is Mine	NAUGHTY MARIETTA	The Owl and the Polecat Antoinette and Anatole Student's Song
	KID MILLIONS	An Earful of Music Okay, Toots When My Ship Comes In Ice Cream Fantasy	RECKLESS	Cyclone
			LAST OF THE PAGANS	Shadows on the Starlit Waters
	OPERATOR 13	Sleepy Head Once in a Lifetime	1936 SAN FRANCISCO	San Francisco The One Love
	HOLLYWOOD PARTY	I've Had My Moments	HER MASTER'S VOICE	With All My Heart
	CARAVAN	Ha-Cha-Cha Happy, I Am Happy Wine Song	LET'S SING AGAIN	Let's Sing Again
			LOVE ON THE RUN	Gone
			ROSE-MARIE	Pardon Me, Madame Just for You
			SMALL TOWN GIRL	Small Town Girl

1937	A DAY AT THE RACES	All God's Chillun Got Rhythm Tomorrow Is Another Day Blue Venetian Waters A Message from the Man in the Moon	
	THEY GAVE HIM A GUN	A Love Song of Long Ago	
	MAYTIME	Farewell to Dreams A Lady Comes to Town Hats in the Air	
	THE FIREFLY	He Who Loves and Runs Away	
	THREE SMART GIRLS	My Heart Is Singing Someone to Care for Me	
	MUSIC FOR MADAME	I Want the World to Know My Sweet Bambino	
	CAPTAINS COURAGEOUS	Don't Cry Little Fish Ooh, What a Terrible Man!	
	THE BRIDE WORE RED	Who Wants Love?	
1938	THE GIRL OF THE GOLDEN WEST	Who Are We to Say Soldiers of Fortune Shadows on the Moon Senorita Sun-up to Sundown The Wind in the Trees The West Ain't Wild Anymore Dream of Love Girl of the Golden West	

	EVERYBODY SING	Swing, Mr. Mendelssohn, Swing Down on Melody Farm The Show Must Go On The Sun Never Sets on Swing Never Was There Such a Perfect Day The One I Love (Will Come Along Some Day)	
1939	HONOLULU	Honolulu This Night Will Be My Souvenir The Leader Doesn't Like Music	
	IDIOT'S DELIGHT	How Strange	
	BROADWAY SERENADE	No Time to Argue Time Changes Everything but Love For Ev'ry Lonely Heart Broadway Serenade	
	BRIDAL SUITE	When I Gave My Smile to You One Little Drink to You	
	BALALAIKA	Beneath the Winter's Snows In a Heart As Brave As Your Own Soldiers of the Czar The Magic of Your Love My Heart Is a Gypsy	
1940	SPRING PARADE	Waltzing in the Clouds When April Sings Blue Danube Dream In a Spring Parade	

LILLIAN RUSSELL	Blue Lovebird		I'm the Guy Who Loves You
THE GOLDEN FLEECING	March, March, the Boys Are Tramping		I Can't Get Along with Horses
BITTERSWEET	Love in Any Language	TWO GIRLS ON BROADWAY	Rancho Santa Fe True Love
GO WEST	Ridin' the Range You Can't Argue with Love As If I Don't Know Go West There's a New Moon over the Old Corral	1941 THE CHOCOLATE SOLDIER ZIEGFELD GIRL	While My Lady Sleeps You Stepped Out of a Dream

Ziegfeld Girl (Metro-Goldwyn-Mayer, 1941).
Museum of Modern Art/Film Stills Archive, New York City.

Courtesy of Jack Gordon

Mack Gordon

The most successful lyric writer in motion picture history was Mack Gordon. Although lyricists Sammy Cahn and Johnny Mercer each received four Academy Awards, neither created as many film songs that achieved national popularity as Gordon. One hundred and fifteen of his songs written for the screen were hits.

Mack Gordon was born in Warsaw, Poland, in 1904. His parents settled in New York City when he was a child, and he entered show business as a boy soprano in a minstrel show. As he gained experience, he developed comedy routines and landed engagements on the vaudeville circuit as a singing comic. The first song with words by Gordon was "Ain'tcha" featured in Paramount's 1929 "talkie" *Pointed Heels*. His work was also heard in the films *Song of Love* (1929) and *Swing High* (1930). In 1930, he and Harold Adamson wrote the lyrics for "Time on My Hands." The number, introduced in Florenz Ziegfeld's musical comedy *Smiles*, became a popular music standard. Its success led to assignments on five more stage musicals on which he collaborated with composer Harry Revel. The team's reputation as Broadway songwriters soon brought them offers from Hollywood.

In 1933, Universal was grooming crooner Russ Columbo as a rival for Paramount's new singing sensation Bing Crosby. The studio cast Columbo in *Broadway thru a Keyhole* and engaged Mack Gordon and Harry Revel to write the score. Their work produced the hits "Doin' the Uptown Lowdown" and "You're My Past, Present and Future." Universal shared Gordon and Revel with the team's home studio, Paramount. The year *Broadway thru a Keyhole* was released, the songwriters had compositions included in Paramount's musical *Sitting Pretty* and its dramatic films *White Woman* and *Design for Living*. During the next two years, Mack Gordon created the lyrics for songs introduced in such films as *We're Not Dressing, Shoot the Works, She Loves Me Not, Two for Tonight, College Rhythm*, and *Stolen Harmony*. His title song for *Paris in the Spring* (1935) was the first of Gordon's numbers to lead "Your Hit Parade." After *Collegiate*, he left Paramount and continued working with Revel at Twentieth Century-Fox.

Mack Gordon had two songs climb to the number one spot on "Your Hit Parade" during his first year at Fox: "Goodnight My Love" and "When I'm with You" introduced by Alice Faye and Shirley Temple in *Stowaway* and *Poor Little Rich Girl*. Among the memorable films he worked on from 1937 through 1939 were *Ali Baba Goes to Town* starring Eddie Cantor; *Wake Up and Live* and *Love and Hisses*, in which columnist Walter Winchell and bandleader Ben Bernie perpetuated their radio feud; *This Is My Affair* starring husband and wife Robert Taylor and Barbara Stanwyck; *Josette* starring French import Simone Simon; and *In Old Chicago* in which the disastrous fire of 1871 was recreated.

Mack Gordon and Harry Revel parted company in 1939. Gordon began collaborating with composer Harry Warren and went on to even greater heights. The new partnership brought the lyricist his first Academy

Award nomination for the song "Down Argentina Way" sung by Betty Grable in *Down Argentine Way* (1940). Additional nominations followed for "Chattanooga Choo Choo" from *Sun Valley·Serenade* (1941) and "I've Got a Gal in Kalamazoo" from *Orchestra Wives* (1942). After ten years as a motion picture songwriter, Mack Gordon won the Best Song Oscar for his words to "You'll Never Know" introduced by Alice Faye in Fox's 1943 musical *Hello, Frisco, Hello*. Working with other composers, Gordon received Oscar bids for "I'm Making Believe" (1944), "I Can't Begin to Tell You" (1945), "You Do" (1947), "Through a Long and Sleepless Night" (1949), and "Wilhelmina" (1950). Nineteen of his songs were featured on the weekly surveys of the nation's ten top tunes during the forties—with seven of them in first place.

Gordon occasionally worked without a collaborator and was responsible for both the music and lyrics for the hit songs "Here Comes Cookie," "My Heart Is an Open Book," and "This Is the Beginning of the End." Mack Gordon was 54 years old at the time of his death in 1959.

Year	Film	Songs	Film	Songs
1929	POINTED HEELS	Ain'tcha?	SHOOT THE WORKS	With My Eyes Wide Open, I'm Dreaming
	SONG OF LOVE	I'm Somebody's Baby Now		Were Your Ears Burning, Baby?
		I'm Walking with the Moonbeams		
		White Way Blues	COLLEGE RHYTHYM	Stay as Sweet as You Are
1930	SWING HIGH	Do You Think I Could Grow on You?		Take a Number from One to Ten
		It Must Be Love		College Rhythm
		With My Guitar and You		Let's Give Three Cheers for Love
1933	BROADWAY THRU A KEYHOLE	You're My Past, Present and Future		Goo Goo (I'm Ga-Ga Over You)
		Doin' the Uptown Lowdown		
		I Love You Pizzicato	SHE LOVES ME NOT	Straight from the Shoulder
		When You Were the Girl on a Scooter and I Was the Boy on a Bike		I'm Hummin', I'm Whistlin', I'm Singin'
				Put a Little Rhythm in Every Little Thing You Do
	SITTING PRETTY	Did You Ever See a Dream Walking		
		You're Such a Comfort to Me	THE OLD-FASHIONED WAY	Rolling in Love
		Good Morning Glory		A Little Bit of Heaven Known as Mother
		Ballad of the South		
		I Wanna Meander with Miranda	HERE COMES THE GROOM	I'll Blame the Waltz, Not You
		Many Moons Ago		
		Lucky Little Extra	1935	LOVE IN BLOOM	Here Comes Cookie
		There's a Bluebird at My Window		My Heart Is an Open Book
		And Then We Wrote		Got Me Doin' Things
		Lights, Action, Camera, Love		Let Me Sing You to Sleep with a Love Song
	WHITE WOMAN	Yes, My Dear	PARIS IN THE SPRING	Paris in the Spring
		He's a Cute Brute		Bon Jour, Mam'selle
				Why Do They Call It Gay Paree?
	DESIGN FOR LIVING	My Design for Living		Jealousy
1934	THE GAY DIVORCEE	Don't Let It Bother You	TWO FOR TONIGHT	From the Top of Your Head to the Tip of Your Toes
		Let's K-nock K-nees		Without a Word of Warning
	WE'RE NOT DRESSING	Love Thy Neighbor		Takes Two to Make a Bargain
		Once in a Blue Moon		I Wish I Were Aladdin
		May I?		Two for Tonight
		She Reminds Me of You		
		Goodnight, Lovely Little Lady	STOLEN HARMONY	Would There Be Love?
		It's the Animal in Me		Let's Spill the Beans
				I Never Had a Man to Cry Over
				Fagin, You'se a Viper

1936	COLLEGIATE	I Feel Like a Feather in the Breeze	WAKE UP AND LIVE	Never in a Million Years
		You Hit the Spot		There's a Lull in My Life
		Rhythmatic		Wake Up and Live
		My Grandfather's Clock in the Hallway		I'm Bubbling Over
		Who Am I?		It's Swell of You
		Will I Ever Know?		Oh, but I'm Happy
		Guess Again		I Love You Too Much, Muchacha
		Learn to Be Lovely	LOVE AND HISSES	Sweet Someone
	POOR LITTLE RICH GIRL	When I'm with You		I Wanna Be in Winchell's Column
		Oh, My Goodness		Broadway's Gone Hawaiian
		You've Gotta Eat Your Spinach, Baby		Be a Good Sport
		But Definitely		Lost in Your Eyes
		Buy a Bar of Barry's	ALI BABA GOES TO TOWN	I've Got My Heart Set on You
		I Like a Military Man		Laugh Your Way through Life
	STOWAWAY	Goodnight My Love		Swing Is Here to Sway
		One Never Knows, Does One?		Vote for Honest Abe
		You Gotta S-M-I-L-E to Be H-A-Double-P-Y		Arabania
		I Wanna Go to the Zoo	EVERYBODY DANCE	My What a Different Night!
		A Dreamland Choo-Choo to Lullaby Town		Everybody Dance
				What Does It Get Me?
	FLORIDA SPECIAL	It's You I'm Talkin' About		Why Did I Marry a Wrestler?
1937	HEAD OVER HEELS	Through the Courtesy of Love	1938 IN OLD CHICAGO	In Old Chicago
		May I Have the Next Romance with You?	MY LUCKY STAR	I've Got a Date with a Dream
		Lookin' Around Corners for You		Could You Pass in Love?
		Head over Heels in Love		By a Wishing Well
		There's That Look in Your Eyes		This May Be the Night
		Don't Give a Good Gosh Darn		The All American Swing
	YOU CAN'T HAVE EVERYTHING	Please Pardon Us, We're in Love	LOVE FINDS ANDY HARDY	Meet the Beat of My Heart
		Afraid to Dream		What Do You Know about Love?
		The Loveliness of You		It Never Rains but What it Pours
		You Can't Have Everything		
		Danger—Love at Work	SALLY, IRENE AND MARY	Sweet as a Song
	THIS IS MY AFFAIR	I Hum a Waltz		Got My Mind on Music
		Fill It Up	JOSETTE	Where in the World?
		Put Down Your Glass		In Any Language
	THIN ICE	I'm Olga from the Volga		May I Drop a Petal in Your Glass of Wine?

	REBECCA OF SUNNYBROOK FARM	An Old Straw Hat
	THANKS FOR EVERYTHING	Thanks for Everything You're the World's Fairest Three Cheers for Henry Smith Puff-a-Puff
	I'LL GIVE A MILLION	Fond of You
	HOLD THAT CO-ED	Here Am I Doing It Hold That Co-ed
1939	ROSE OF WASHINGTON SQUARE	I Never Knew Heaven Could Speak
	TAILSPIN	Are You in the Mood for Mischief?
	THE RAINS CAME	The Rains Came
1940	DOWN ARGENTINE WAY	Down Argentina Way Two Dreams Met Nenita Sing to Your Senorita
	TIN PAN ALLEY	You Say the Sweetest Things, Baby
	YOUNG PEOPLE	I Wouldn't Take a Million Mason-Dixon Line Fifth Avenue Young People Tra-La-La-La
	STAR DUST	Secrets in the Moonlight Don't Let It Get You Down
	JOHNNY APOLLO	This Is the Beginning of the End
	LITTLE OLD NEW YORK	In an Old Dutch Garden Who Is the Beau of the Belle of New York?
	LILLIAN RUSSELL	Adored One Waltz Is King

1941	SUN VALLEY SERENADE	Chattanooga Choo Choo I Know Why It Happened in Sun Valley The Kiss Polka
	THAT NIGHT IN RIO	I Yi Yi Yi Yi Chica Chica Boom Chic They Met in Rio Boa Noite
	WEEKEND IN HAVANNA	Tropical Magic Weekend in Havana Man with the Lollipop Song The Nango When I Love I Love Romance and Rhumba
	THE GREAT AMERICAN BROADCAST	I've Got a Bone to Pick with You I Take to You It's All in a Lifetime Long Ago Last Night Where Are You? The Great American Broadcast
1942	ORCHESTRA WIVES	I've Got a Gal in Kalamazoo That's Sabotage Serenade in Blue At Last People Like You and Me
	SPRINGTIME IN THE ROCKIES	I Had the Craziest Dream A Poem Set to Music Pan-American Jubilee Run, Little Raindrop, Run
	SON OF FURY	Blue Tahitian Moon
	ICELAND	There Will Never Be Another You You Can't Say No to a Soldier Let's Bring New Glory to Old Glory I Like a Military Tune
	SONG OF THE ISLANDS	Blue Shadows and White Gardenias O'Brien Has Gone Hawaiian Maluna, Malalo, Mawaena What's Buzzin'-Cousin? Down on Ami Ami Oni Oni Isle Sing Me a Song of the Islands

1943	HELLO, FRISCO, HELLO	You'll Never Know
	SWEET ROSIE O'GRADY	My Heart Tells Me
		The Wishing Waltz
		Get Your Police Gazette
		My Sam
		Goin' to the County Fair
		Where, Oh Where, Oh Where Is the Groom?
1944	SWEET AND LOWDOWN	I'm Making Believe
		Hey, Bub, Let's Have a Ball
		Ten Days with Baby
		One Chord in Two Flats
		Tsk, Tsk, That's Love
		Chug-Chug, Choo-Choo, Chug
	GREENWICH VILLAGE	I Like to Be Loved by You
	PIN-UP GIRL	Time Alone Will Tell
		Once Too Often
		You're My Little Pin-Up Girl
		Yankee Doodle Hayride
		The Story of the Very Merry Widow
		Don't Carry Tales Out of School
		Red Robins, Bob Whites and Bluebirds
	IRISH EYES ARE SMILING	Bessie in a Bustle
		I Don't Want a Million Dollars
1945	THE DOLLY SISTERS	I Can't Begin to Tell You
		Don't Be Too Old-Fashioned (Old-Fashioned Girl)
		We Have Been Around
		Powder, Lipstick and Rouge

	DIAMOND HORSESHOE	The More I See You
		I Wish I Knew
		In Acapulco
		Play Me an Old-Fashioned Melody
		A Nickel's Worth of Jive
		The Mink Lament
		Welcome to the Diamond Horseshoe
		Cooking Up a Show
1946	THREE LITTLE GIRLS IN BLUE	You Make Me Feel So Young
		Somewhere in the Night
		On the Boardwalk in Atlantic City
		Always the Lady
		Three Little Girls in Blue
		I Like Mike
		A Farmer's Life Is a Very Merry Life
	THE RAZOR'S EDGE	Mam'selle
1947	MOTHER WORE TIGHTS	You Do
		Kokomo, Indiana
		On a Little Two-Seat Tandem
		This Is My Favorite City
		There's Nothing Like a Song
		Fare-Thee-Well Dear Alma Mater
	DAISY KENYON	You Can't Run Away from Love
1948	WHEN MY BABY SMILES AT ME	By the Way
		What Did I Do?
1949	COME TO THE STABLE	Through a Long and Sleepless Night
	THE BEAUTIFUL BLONDE FROM BASHFUL BEND	Everytime I Meet You
	IT HAPPENS EVERY SPRING	It Happens Every Spring

1950	WABASH AVENUE	Wilhelmina
		Baby, Won't You Say You Love Me?
		Clean Up Chicago
		Down on Wabash Avenue
		May I Tempt You with a Big Red Rosy Apple?
	SUMMER STOCK	If You Feel Like Singing, Sing
		Friendly Star
		Happy Harvest
		Dig-Dig-Dig for Your Dinner
	UNDER MY SKIN	Stranger in the Night
1951	CALL ME MISTER	I Just Can't Do Enough for You—Baby
		Japanese Girl Like 'merican Boy
		Love Is Back in Business
	I LOVE MELVIN	Life Has Its Funny Little Ups and Downs
		I Wanna Wander
		We Have Never Met as Yet
		A Lady Loves
		Where Did You Learn to Dance?
		And There You Are
		Saturday Afternoon before the Game

1953	THE GIRL NEXT DOOR	Nowhere Guy
		The Girl Next Door
		You
		If I Love You a Mountain
1954	YOUNG AT HEART	You, My Love
1956	BUNDLE OF JOY	All about Love
		Worry about Tomorrow—Tomorrow
		What's So Good About Good Morning?
		Some Day Soon
		Lullaby in Blue
		I Never Felt This Way Before
		Bundle of Joy

134

Weekend in Havana (Twentieth Century-Fox, 1941).
Roy Bishop Collection .

Harold Adamson

Harold Adamson would probably have preferred acting in motion pictures to writing songs for them. Although he experimented with verse writing while in prep school, his ambition was to become a thespian. While a student at the University of Kansas, he gained experience on the boards by performing in summer stock. On transferring to Harvard University, he landed roles in the Hasty Pudding Club Shows. Like many artists who had trained for other careers, his plans were changed by the unexpected success of a song. In Adamson's case, the composition was "Time on My Hands" for which he wrote the lyrics in conjunction with Mack Gordon. Adamson was barely out of college when the song was introduced in Florenz Ziegfeld's Broadway production *Smiles* in 1930. That same year, his work was heard in *Earl Carroll's Vanities*. After three more stage musicals, the 27-year-old lyricist was lured to the cinema capital by an offer from Metro-Goldwyn-Mayer.

One of the most popular stars under contract to MGM was Joan Crawford. Miss Crawford had danced in the chorus of Broadway musicals before entering films and had gained a reputation for her footwork in such pictures as *Our Dancing Daughters, Hollywood Revue of 1929*, and *Dance, Fools, Dance*. Harold Adamson's first assignment for the studio was Crawford's *Dancing Lady* (1933) co-starring Clark Gable. The film's score included numbers by other lyricists, but it was Adamson's "Everything I Have Is Yours" that audiences remembered. The next year, he worked on Fox's *Bottoms Up* starring Spencer Tracy; on RKO's *Strictly Dynamite*, in which Lupe Velez and Jimmy Durante appeared; and, working on loan to United Artists, on the Eddie Cantor vehicle *Kid Millions*.

The first of Adamson's songs to place on the new radio program called "Your Hit Parade" was "Ev'rything's Been Done Before" sung by Jean Harlow in the 1935 release *Reckless*. Harlow also introduced "Did I Remember" which was nominated for the Academy Award in 1936. Both "Did I Remember" (from *Suzy*) and Adamson's "You" (from *The Great Ziegfeld*) rose to the top of "Your Hit Parade." After a dozen films at MGM, Harold Adamson signed with Universal, where he supplied Alice Faye and Deanna Durbin with two more "Hit Parade" favorites—"You're a Sweetheart" and "My Own," which brought the lyricist his second bid for the Oscar in 1938. During the years of World War II, Adamson's film songs "I Couldn't Sleep a Wink Last Night," "A Lovely Way to Spend an Evening," "Daybreak," "How Blue the Night," and "I Don't Care Who Knows It" all made the weekly surveys of America's ten top tunes. He competed in the annual Oscar derbys for the third and fourth times when "Change of Heart" (from *Hit Parade of 1943*) and "I Couldn't Sleep a Wink Last Night" (from *Higher and Higher*) were in the running.

Adamson's success continued after the war and he provided lyrics for Susan Hayward in *Smash-Up* (1947), Jane Powell in *A Date with Judy* (1948), Jane Russell in

His Kind of Woman (1951), and Marilyn Monroe in *Gentlemen Prefer Blondes* (1953). In 1956, he added words to Victor Young's main theme from *Around the World in 80 Days*, and it became the eighth of his inventions to top "Your Hit Parade." He received his fifth Academy Award nomination for the title song for *An Affair to Remember* in 1957.

Harold Adamson was born in Greenville, New Jersey, in 1906 and was 73 at the time of his death in 1980.

The Film Songs of Harold Adamson

1933	DANCING LADY	Everything I Have Is Yours Let's Go Bavarian
	TURN BACK THE CLOCK	Tony's Wife
1934	BOTTOMS UP	Little Did I Dream Turn on the Moon Throwin' My Love Away
	PALOOKA	Like Me a Little Bit Less (Love Me a Little Bit More)
	KID MILLIONS	Your Head on My Shoulder I Want to Be a Minstrel Man
	COMING OUT PARTY	I Think You're Wonderful
	STRICTLY DYNAMITE	Swing It, Sister Oh Me, Oh My, Oh You
	LONG LOST FATHER	It Isn't So Much That I Wouldn't
	THE BAND PLAYS ON	Roll Up the Score
1935	SHADOW OF A DOUBT	Beyond the Shadow of a Doubt
	FOLIES BERGERE	You Took the Words Right Out of My Mouth
	RECKLESS	Ev'rything's Been Done Before Hear What My Heart Is Saying Trocadero
	HERE COMES THE BAND	Tender Is the Night I'm Bound for Heaven The Army Band
	THE PERFECT GENTLEMAN	It's Only Human
1936	SUZY	Did I Remember
	THE GREAT ZIEGFELD	You You Never Looked So Beautiful You Gotta Pull Strings Queen of the Jungle She's a Follies Girl
	BANJO ON MY KNEE	There's Something in the Air Where the Lazy River Goes By With a Banjo on My Knee
	THE VOICE OF BUGLE ANN	There's a Home in the Mountains
	PICCADILLY JIM	Night of Nights
	HIS BROTHER'S WIFE	Can't We Fall in Love?
1937	HITTING A NEW HIGH	I Hit a New High Let's Give Love Another Chance This Never Happened Before You're Like a Song
	YOU'RE A SWEETHEART	You're a Sweetheart My Fine Feathered Friend Broadway Jamboree Who Killed Maggie? Oh, Oh Oklahoma
	TOP OF THE TOWN	There's No Two Ways about It Where Are You? That Foolish Feeling Top of the Town Blame It on the Rhumba Jamboree Fireman, Fireman, Save My Child Post Office (I've Got to Be Kissed)
	MERRY-GO-ROUND OF 1938	You're My Dish More Power to You I'm in My Glory Six of One, Half a Dozen of the Other The Grand Street Comedy Four
	WHEN LOVE IS YOUNG	When Love Is Young Did Anyone Ever Tell You?
	BREEZING HOME	You're in My Heart Again I'm Hittin' the Hot Spots
1938	MAD ABOUT MUSIC	I Love to Whistle Chapel Bells A Serenade to the Stars There Isn't a Day Goes By
	THAT CERTAIN AGE	My Own You're as Pretty as a Picture That Certain Age Be a Good Scout Has Anyone Ever Told You Before?

	YOUTH TAKES A FLING	For the First Time Heigh-Ho the Merry-O	
	ROAD TO RENO	Ridin' Home I Gave My Heart Away Tonight Is the Night	
	DEVIL'S PARTY	Things Are Coming My Way	
	RECKLESS LIVING	When the Stars Go to Sleep	
1939	THE FAMILY NEXT DOOR	It's a Dog's Life	
1940	RIDE, TENDERFOOT, RIDE	The Woodpecker Song	
1941	HOLD THAT GHOST	Aurora	
1943	HIGHER AND HIGHER	I Couldn't Sleep a Wink Last Night A Lovely Way to Spend an Evening The Music Stopped Higher and Higher It's a Most Important Affair You're on Your Own Minuet in Boogie I Saw You First Today I'm a Debutante Mrs. Whiffen	
	THOUSANDS CHEER	Daybreak	
	FOLLOW THE BAND	Hilo Hattie	
	HIT PARADE OF 1943	Change of Heart Do These Old Eyes Deceive Me? Harlem Sandman That's How to Write a Song Who Took Me Home Last Night? Tahm Boom Bah	

	AROUND THE WORLD	Don't Believe Everything You Dream Candlelight and Wine They Just Chopped Down the Old Apple Tree He's Got a Secret Weapon Great News Is in the Making A Moke from Shamokin Roodle-de-Doo	
1944	SOMETHING FOR THE BOYS	Wouldn't It Be Nice? I Wish We Didn't Have to Say Goodnight In the Middle of Nowhere Eighty Miles Outside Atlanta Boom Brachee Samba Boogie	
	FOUR JILLS IN A JEEP	How Blue the Night You Send Me How Many Times Do I Have to Tell You? Crazy Me Ohio It's the Old Army Game You Never Miss a Trick Heil Heel Hitler	
	TWO GIRLS AND A SAILOR	Thrill of a New Romance	
	THE PRINCESS AND THE PIRATE	How Would You Like to Kiss Me in the Moonlight?	
	BATHING BEAUTY	I'll Take the High Note	
1945	DOLL FACE	Here Comes Heaven Again Hubba, Hubba, Hubba (Dig Ya Later) Red Hot and Beautiful Somebody's Walkin' in My Dreams Chico Chico	

	NOB HILL	I Don't Care Who Knows It I Walked In (with My Eyes Wide Open) San Francisco		IF YOU KNEW SUSIE	Livin' the Life of Love My How the Time Goes By What Do I Want with Money?

NOB HILL — I Don't Care Who Knows It / I Walked In (with My Eyes Wide Open) / San Francisco

BRING ON THE GIRLS — Bring on the Girls / Uncle Sammy Hit Miami / How Would You Like to Take My Picture? / You Moved Right In / It Could Happen to Me / True to the Navy / I'm Gonna Hate Myself in the Morning

1946 DO YOU LOVE ME? — I Didn't Mean a Word I Said

1947 BIG TOWN — It's a Small World

SMASH-UP — Life Can Be Beautiful / I Miss That Feeling / Hush-a-Bye Island

CALENDAR GIRL — I'm Telling You Now / Lovely Night to Go Dancing / Calendar Girl / At the Fireman's Ball / A Bluebird Is Singing to Me / New York's a Nice Place to Visit / Let's Have Some Pretzels and Beer

HIT PARADE OF 1947 — I Guess I'll Have That Dream Right Away / I Threw a Kiss to a Star / Chiquita from Santa Anita / Is There Anyone Here from Texas? / Couldn't Be More in Love / The Customer Is Always Wrong / The Cats Are Going to the Dogs

1948 A DATE WITH JUDY — It's a Most Unusual Day

IF YOU KNEW SUSIE — Livin' the Life of Love / My How the Time Goes By / What Do I Want with Money?

1951 HIS KIND OF WOMAN — You'll Know

1952 THE LAS VEGAS STORY — My Resistance Is Low

1953 GENTLEMEN PREFER BLONDES — When Love Goes Wrong / Ain't There Anyone Here for Love?

1954 THE LEGIONNAIRE — Montmartre

1955 JUPITER'S DARLING — I Never Trust a Woman / I Have a Dream / The Life of an Elephant / Horatio's Narration / If This be Slav'ry / Don't Let This Night Get Away / Hannibal's Victory March

1957 AN AFFAIR TO REMEMBER — An Affair to Remember / Tomorrowland / The Tiny Scout / Contin-u-e

CHINA GATE — China Gate

FORTY GUNS — God Has His Arms around Me

1958 SEPARATE TABLES — Separate Tables

THE SEVEN HILLS OF ROME — The Seven Hills of Rome

1962 SATAN NEVER SLEEPS — Satan Never Sleeps

1963 A TICKLISH AFFAIR — Love Is a Ticklish Affair

1964 THE INCREDIBLE MR. LIMPET — I Wish I Were a Fish / Hail to Henry Limpet / Be Careful How You Wish / Deep Rapture

Top of the Town (Universal, 1937).
Collectors Book Store, Hollywood, CA.

Courtesy of Mrs. Johnny Mercer

Johnny Mercer

Only three songwriters have received four Academy Awards in the forty-four-year history of the Best Song Oscar. The first four-time winner was Johnny Mercer who was born in Savannah, Georgia, in 1909. After completing high school, Mercer went to New York with the Savannah Little Theatre Group, which was entered in an acting competition. Mercer had started writing lyrics when he was 15, and he continued his songwriting efforts while trying to find work as an actor. Producers were unimpressed with his dramatic ability, but one of them used his song "Out of Breath and Scared to Death of You" in the 1930 edition of *The Garrick Gaieties*. Still determined to become a performer, Mercer joined Paul Whiteman's orchestra as a vocalist. The bandleader introduced Mercer to composer Hoagy Carmichael, and the songwriters collaborated on the 1933 hit "Lazybones." Johnny Mercer's next move was to Hollywood.

Mercer's lyrics first reached the screen in *College Coach* released by Warner Brothers in 1933. The film was followed by *Transatlantic Merry-Go-Round* (1934) and the 1935 musicals *To Beat the Band* and *Old Man Rhythm*, in which Mercer was employed as both lyricist and actor. He then proved his merit as a composer by writing the music as well as the words for "I'm an Old Cowhand" introduced by Bing Crosby in *Rhythm on the Range* (1936). Mercer signed a contract with Warner's, and from 1937 through 1939, he supplied the studio with the "Hit Parade" favorites "Have You Got Any Castles, Baby?," "Too Marvelous for Words," "Jeepers Creepers," "You Must Have Been a Beautiful Baby,"

and "Day Dreaming All Night Long." He was nominated for his first Academy Award for "Jeepers Creepers" sung by Louis Armstrong in *Hard to Get* (1938).

The forties found songs with words by Mercer entered in the "Oscar" race four years in a row when he was nominated for "The Love of My Life" (1940), "I'd Know You Anywhere" (1940), "Blues in the Night" (1941), "Dearly Beloved" (1942), "That Old Black Magic" (1943) and "My Shining Hour" (1943). "Accent-tchu-ate the Positive" was a contender in 1945. Mercer recorded many of his hits for Capitol Records— a company he co-founded in 1942. He worked on the scores for some of the most popular screen musicals of World War II including *Star Spangled Rhythm*, *The Fleet's In*, *Here Come the Waves*, *You Were Never Lovelier*, and *The Sky's the Limit*. The end of the war brought Mercer his initial Academy Award for "On the Atchison, Topeka and the Santa Fe" introduced by Judy Garland in Metro-Goldwyn-Mayer's *The Harvey Girls* (1946). His second win came five years later for "In the Cool, Cool, Cool of the Evening" performed by Bing Crosby and Jane Wyman in Paramount's *Here Comes the Groom*.

Johnny Mercer provided the lyrics for four more productions before screen musicals began their decline in popularity: *The Belle of New York* (1952), *Everything I Have Is Yours* (1952), *Seven Brides for Seven Brothers* (1954), and *Daddy Long Legs* (1955). He worked without a collaborator on *Daddy Long Legs*, and its score earned him an Oscar nomination as both the composer and lyricist of "Something's Gotta Give." His twelfth bid from the Academy came for his words to the title song "The Facts of Life" (1960). In 1961, he teamed with composer Henry Mancini. Their partnership produced the Best Songs of 1961 and 1962—"Moon River" and "The Days of Wine and Roses"—and the Oscar candidates "Charade" (1963), "The Sweetheart Tree" (1965), and "Whistling Away in the Dark" (1969).

Mercer's last nomination was for "Life Is What You Make It" from the 1971 release *Kotch*.

During his forty year career as a motion picture songwriter, Johnny Mercer also contributed to ten musicals staged on Broadway, including the 1951 production *Top Banana* for which he wrote both words and music. In 1975, he was operated on for a brain tumor, an operation from which he never recovered. The winner of four of Hollywood's Best Song Oscars died in 1976 at the age of 66.

1933	COLLEGE COACH	What Will I Do without You?
1934	TRANSATLANTIC MERRY-GO-ROUND	If I Had a Million Dollars
1935	TO BEAT THE BAND	If You Were Mine I Saw Her at Eight O'Clock Eeny Meeny Miney Mo Meet Miss America Santa Claus Came in the Spring
	OLD MAN RHYTHM	I Never Saw a Better Night Old Man Rhythm There's Nothing like a College Education Boys Will Be Boys When You Are in My Arms Comes the Revolution, Baby
1936	RHYTHM ON THE RANGE	I'm an Old Cowhand
1937	VARSITY SHOW	Have You Got Any Castles, Baby? We're Working Our Way through College Love Is on the Air Tonight You've Got Something There Moonlight on the Campus Old King Cole On with the Dance When Your College Days Are Gone
	HOLLYWOOD HOTEL	Hooray for Hollywood I'm Like a Fish Out of Water I've Hitched My Wagon to a Star Let That Be a Lesson to You Silhouetted in the Moonlight Can't Teach My Old Heart New Tricks Sing You Son of a Gun
	THE SINGING MARINE	Night over Shanghai
	READY, WILLING AND ABLE	Too Marvelous for Words Just a Quiet Evening Sentimental and Melancholy

1938	GOING PLACES	Jeepers Creepers Say It with a Kiss Mutiny in the Nursery Oh, What a Horse Was Charlie
	HARD TO GET	You Must Have Been a Beautiful Baby There's a Sunny Side to Every Situation
	COWBOY FROM BROOKLYN	Ride, Tenderfoot, Ride I'll Dream Tonight I've Got a Heartful of Music Cowboy from Brooklyn
	GARDEN OF THE MOON	The Lady on the Two Cent Stamp The Girl Friend of a Whirling Dervish Confidentially Love Is Where You Find It Garden of the Moon
	GOLD DIGGERS IN PARIS	Day Dreaming All Night Long
1939	NAUGHTY BUT NICE	Hooray for Spinach In a Moment of Weakness Corn Pickin' I'm Happy about the Whole Thing
	WINGS OF THE NAVY	Wings over the Navy
1940	SECOND CHORUS	The Love of My Life (I Ain't Hep to That Step but I'll) Dig It Poor Mr. Chisholm Me and the Ghost Upstairs
	YOU'LL FIND OUT	I'd Know You Anywhere You've Got Me This Way I've Got a One Track Mind (Ting-a-Ling) The Bad Humor Man Like the Fella Once Said Don't Think It Ain't Been Charming
	LET'S MAKE MUSIC	Central Park
1941	BLUES IN THE NIGHT	Blues in the Night This Time the Dream's on Me Says Who? Says You, Says I! Hang on to Your Lids, Kids

	YOU'RE THE ONE	I Could Kiss You for That
		You're the One for Me
		Strawberry Lane
		Gee, I Wish I'd Listened to
		    My Mother
		The Yogi (Who Lost His
		    Will Power)	

	NAVY BLUES	In Waikiki You're a Natural Navy Blues When Are We Going to Land Abroad?	
	BIRTH OF THE BLUES	The Walter and the Porter and the Upstairs Maid	

1942	STAR SPANGLED
	    RHYTHM
		That Old Black Magic
		Hit the Road to Dreamland
		I'm Doing It for Defense
		Old Glory
		A Sweater a Sarong and a
		    Peek-a-boo Bang
		Sharp as a Tack
		On the Swing Shift
		He Loved Me Till the
		    All-Clear Came	

	ALL THROUGH THE NIGHT	All through the Night	
	CAPTAINS OF THE CLOUDS	Captains of the Clouds	
	YOU WERE NEVER LOVELIER	Dearly Beloved I'm Old-Fashioned You Were Never Lovelier Wedding in the Spring On the Beam The "Shorty George"	

	THE FLEET'S IN	Tangerine
		I Remember You
		Not Mine
		If You Build a Better
		    Mousetrap
		Arthur Murray Taught Me
		    Dancing in a Hurry
		When You Hear the Time
		    Signal
		The Fleet's In
		Tomorrow You Belong to
		    Uncle Sam	

1943	THE SKY'S THE LIMIT	My Shining Hour
		One for My Baby
		I've Got a Lot in Common
		    with You
		Harvey, the Victory
		    Garden Man	

	TRUE TO LIFE	The Old Music Master There She Was Mister Pollyanna Sudsy Suds Theme Song	
	THEY GOT ME COVERED	Palsy Walsy	

1944	HERE COME THE WAVES	Ac-cent-tchu-ate the
		    Positive
		I Promise You
		Let's Take the Long Way
		    Home
		There's a Fellow Waitin' in
		    Poughkeepsie
		My Mamma Thinks I'm a
		    Star
		Here Come the Waves	

	TO HAVE AND HAVE NOT	How Little We Know	
1945	OUT OF THIS WORLD	Out of This World June Comes Around Every Year	

1946	THE HARVEY GIRLS	On the Atchison, Topeka
		    and the Santa Fe
		Wait and See
		It's a Great Big World
		The Wild, Wild West
		In the Valley (Where the
		    Evenin' Sun Goes Down)
		Swing Your Partner Round
		    and Round	

	CENTENNIAL SUMMER	Two Hearts Are Better Than One	
1947	DEAR RUTH	Fine Things	
1948	MR. PEABODY AND THE MERMAID	The Caribees	
1949	MAKE BELIEVE BALLROOM	Make Believe Ballroom	
	ALWAYS LEAVE THEM LAUGHING	Clink Your Glasses	
1950	THE PETTY GIRL	Fancy Free Ah Loves Ya Calypso Song The Petty Girl	

1951	HERE COMES THE
	    GROOM
		In the Cool, Cool, Cool of
		    the Evening	

	MY FAVORITE SPY	I Wind Up Taking a Fall	

Seven Brides for Seven Brothers (Metro-Goldwyn-Mayer, 1954).
Collectors Book Store, Hollywood, CA.

| 1952 | THE BELLE OF NEW YORK | When I'm Out with Belle of New York
Oops!
Naughty but Nice
Bachelor Dinner Song
Baby Doll
A Bride's Wedding-Day Song
Seeing's Believing
I Wanna Be a Dancin' Man
I Want to Beat a Big Bass Drum |
| | THOSE REDHEADS FROM SEATTLE | I Guess It Was You All the Time |

1953	DANGEROUS WHEN WET	Ain't Nature Grand? In My Wildest Dreams I Like Men Liquapep I Got Out of Bed on the Right Side
	EVERYTHING I HAVE IS YOURS	Derry Down Dilly
1954	SEVEN BRIDES FOR SEVEN BROTHERS	Bless Yore Beautiful Hide Wonderful, Wonderful Day Goin' Co'tin' Sobbin' Women Spring, Spring, Spring Lonesome Polecat June Bride When You're in Love

1955	DADDY LONG LEGS	Something's Gotta Give	
		Sluefoot	
		History of the Beat	
		Welcome Egghead	
		C-A-T Spells Cat	
	TIMBERJACK	He's Dead but He Won't Lie Down	
	I'LL CRY TOMORROW	I'll Cry Tomorrow	
1956	YOU CAN'T RUN AWAY FROM IT	You Can't Run Away from It	
		Temporarily	
		Thumbin' a Ride	
		Howdy Friends and Neighbors	
		It Happened One Night	
	SPRING REUNION	Spring Reunion	
	LI'L ABNER	Otherwise	
1957	MISSOURI TRAVELER	The Piney Woods	
1958	LOVE IN THE AFTERNOON	Ariane	
		Love in the Afternoon	
	BERNARDINE	Bernardine	
		Technique	
	MERRY ANDREW	Everything Is Ticketty-Boo	
		Pipes of Pan	
		Chin Up—Stout Fellow	
		Buona Fortuna	
		The Square of the Hypotenuse	
		You Can't Always Have What You Want	
1960	FACTS OF LIFE	The Facts of Life	
1961	BREAKFAST AT TIFFANY'S	Moon River	✓
1962	DAYS OF WINE AND ROSES	The Days of Wine and Roses	✓
	HATARI!	Just for Tonight	
	HOW THE WEST WAS WON	Raise a Ruckus	
		What Was Your Name in the States?	
	MR. HOBBS TAKES A VACATION	Cream Puff	
1963	CHARADE	Charade	
	LOVE WITH THE PROPER STRANGER	Love with the Proper Stranger	

1964	THE PINK PANTHER	It Had Better Be Tonight
	THE AMERICANIZATION OF EMILY	Emily
	MAN'S FAVORITE SPORT?	Man's Favorite Sport?
1965	THE GREAT RACE	The Sweetheart Tree
		He Shouldn't-a, Hadn't-a, Oughtn't-a Swang on Me
	JOHNNY TIGER	World of My Heart
1966	MOMENT TO MOMENT	Moment to Moment
	NOT WITH MY WIFE, YOU DON'T	Big Beautiful Ball
		My Inamorata
	ALVAREZ KELLY	The Ballad of Alvarez Kelly
	A BIG HAND FOR THE LITTLE LADY	Mirror, Mirror, Mirror
1967	BAREFOOT IN THE PARK	Barefoot in the Park
1968	ROSIE	Rosie
1969	DARLING LILI	Whistling Away in the Dark
		The Little Birds
		The Girl in No Man's Land
		Gypsy Violin
		I'll Give You Three Guesses
		Darling Lili
		Smile Away Each Rainy Day
		Skal
		Your Good-Will Ambassador
1971	KOTCH	Life Is What You Make It
1972	ROBIN HOOD	The Phoney King of England
1973	THE LONG GOODBYE	The Long Goodbye

Courtesy of Mrs. Reni Schulman

Harry Revel

Harry Revel

Although all the major studios began signing composers and lyricists to contracts in 1929, none of them could match the stable of songwriters assembled by Paramount. More of the men who eventually became the great songwriters of Hollywood began their motion picture careers at Paramount than at any other studio. In 1929, Paramount's roster included Sam Coslow, Richard Whiting, and Leo Robin. By 1931, Ralph Rainger was on the lot, and the next year the studio acquired the services of Harry Revel.

Revel was born in London in 1895. He was only 15 years old when he was hired to play the piano in a Paris band. During the next decade, he traveled throughout the continent fulfilling engagements with various dance orchestras. While earning his living as a pianist, Revel composed the score for an operetta staged in Berlin. He then interested English showman Andre Charlot in some of his songs, which the producer used in a London revue in 1927. Two years later, the composer sailed for the United States. Revel was 26 when his music was accepted for three Broadway productions in 1931, including the last edition of *The Follies* staged by Florenz Ziegfeld. Two more legitimate musicals followed before Revel was invited to join Paramount.

Most composers and lyricists were paired by the studio after they had signed their contracts. Harry Revel was an exception since Paramount brought both the composer and his Broadway lyricist, Mack Gordon, to the West Coast as a team. For five years, Gordon wrote the words for all of Revel's compositions. The first of Revel's hit melodies for Paramount was "Did You Ever See a Dream Walking" introduced in *Sitting Pretty* in 1933. The following year, Revel supplied Bing Crosby with "Love Thy Neighbor" for *We're Not Dressing*, Lanny Ross with "Stay as Sweet as You Are" for *College Rhythm*, and Dorothy Dell with "With My Eyes Wide Open, I'm Dreaming" for *Shoot the Works*. The first year of the broadcasts of "Your Hit Parade" found three of Revel's numbers on the weekly surveys: "From the Top of Your Head to the Tip of Your Toes" and "Without a Word of Warning," both written for *Two for Tonight* (1935), and the title number from *Paris in the Spring* (1935), which became the nation's number one song. The film *Collegiate* (1936) featured two more Revel melodies that made the "Hit Parade:" "You Hit the Spot" and "I Feel Like a Feather in the Breeze."

When Harry Revel left Paramount to join Twentieth Century-Fox, Mack Gordon went with him. The film industry's top box office attraction was also employed at Fox, and Revel provided Shirley Temple with "When I'm with You" for *Poor Little Rich Girl* and "Goodnight My Love" for *Stowaway*. The pictures were released in 1936, and both songs became number one on "Your Hit Parade." Fox loaned Revel to Gaumont British Studios in 1937 to create the score for *Head over Heels* in which English musical star Jessie Matthews appeared. The performer most closely associated with the composer was Alice Faye who introduced six of his "Hit Parade" favorites from 1937 through 1939: "Afraid to Dream," "Never in a Million Years," "There's a Lull in My Life,"

"Sweet Someone," "Sweet as a Song," and "I Never Knew Heaven Could Speak."

Despite their phenomenal success as a team, Harry Revel and Mack Gordon ended their professional relationship in 1939. During the rest of his career, Revel teamed primarily with lyricists Mort Greene and Paul Francis Webster. The films on which he worked from 1940 through 1952 produced only five successful compositions. Even "When There's a Breeze on Lake Louise" and "Remember Me to Carolina" were quickly forgotten despite being nominated for Academy Awards in 1942 and 1944. In 1947, he became his own lyricist writing both words and music for most of the songs featured in *It Happened on Fifth Avenue*.

Throughout World War II, Harry Revel organized recreation centers for military personnel and staged numerous variety shows for the entertainment of the troops. He died in 1958 at the age of 52.

1933	SITTING PRETTY	Did You Ever See a Dream Walking ✓
		Good Morning Glory
		You're Such a Comfort to Me
		Ballad of the South
		I Wanna Meander with Miranda
		Many Moons Ago ✓
		Lucky Little Extra
		There's a Bluebird at My Window
		And Then We Wrote
		Lights, Action, Camera, Love
	BROADWAY THRU A KEYHOLE	You're My Past, Present and Future
		Doin' the Uptown Lowdown
		I Love You Pizzicato
		When You Were the Girl on a Scooter and I Was the Boy on a Bike
	DESIGN FOR LIVING	My Design for Living
1934	THE GAY DIVORCEE	Don't Let It Bother You ✓
		Let's K-nock K-nees
	WE'RE NOT DRESSING	Love Thy Neighbor
		Once in a Blue Moon
		May I?
		Goodnight, Lovely Little Lady
		She Reminds Me of You
		It's the Animal in Me
	SHOOT THE WORKS	With My Eyes Wide Open I'm Dreaming ✓
		Were Your Ears Burning, Baby?
	COLLEGE RHYTHM	Stay as Sweet as You Are ✓
		Take a Number from One to Ten
		College Rhythm
		Let's Give Three Cheers for Love
		Goo Goo (I'm Ga-ga Over You)
	SHE LOVES ME NOT	Straight from the Shoulder
		I'm Hummin', I'm Whistlin', I'm Singin'
		Put a Little Rhythm in Every Little Thing You Do

	THE OLD-FASHIONED WAY	Rolling in Love
		A Little Bit of Heaven Known as Mother
	HERE COMES THE GROOM	I'll Blame the Waltz, Not You
1935	LOVE IN BLOOM	Let Me Sing You to Sleep with a Love Song
	PARIS IN THE SPRING	Paris in the Spring
		Bon Jour Mam'selle
		Why Do They Call It Gay Paree?
		Jealousy
	TWO FOR TONIGHT	From the Top of Your Head to the Tip of Your Toes
		Without a Word of Warning
		Takes Two to Make a Bargain
		Two for Tonight
		I Wish I Were Aladdin
	STOLEN HARMONY	Would There Be Love?
		Let's Spill the Beans
		I Never Had a Man to Cry Over
		Fagin, You'se a Viper
1936	COLLEGIATE	You Hit the Spot
		I Feel Like a Feather in the Breeze
		Rhythmatic
		My Grandfather's Clock in the Hallway
		Who Am I?
		Will I Ever Know?
		Guess Again
		Learn to Be Lovely
	POOR LITTLE RICH GIRL	When I'm with You
		Oh, My Goodness
		You've Gotta Eat Your Spinach, Baby
		But Definitely
		Buy a Bar of Barry's
		I Like a Military Man
	STOWAWAY	Goodnight My Love ✓
		One Never Knows, Does One? ✓
		You Gotta S-M-I-L-E to be H-A-Double-P-Y
		I Wanna Go to the Zoo
		A Dreamland Choo-Choo to Lullaby Town
	FLORIDA SPECIAL	It's You I'm Talkin' About

1937	HEAD OVER HEELS	Through the Courtesy of Love		ALI BABA GOES TO TOWN	I've Got My Heart Set on You
		May I Have the Next Romance with You?			Laugh Your Way through Life
		Lookin' around Corners for You			Swing Is Here to Sway
		Head over Heels in Love			Vote for Honest Abe
		There's That Look in Your Eyes			Arabania
		Don't Give a Good Gosh Darn		THIS IS MY AFFAIR	I Hum a Waltz
					Fill It Up
	YOU CAN'T HAVE EVERYTHING	Afraid to Dream			Put Down Your Glass
		The Loveliness of You		EVERYBODY DANCE	My What a Different Night!
		You Can't Have Everything			Everybody Dance
		Please Pardon Us, We're in Love			What Does It Get Me?
		Danger—Love at Work			Why Did I Marry a Wrestler?
	WAKE UP AND LIVE	Never in a Million Years		THIN ICE	I'm Olga from the Volga
		There's a Lull in My Life	1938	IN OLD CHICAGO	In Old Chicago
		I'm Bubbling Over		MY LUCKY STAR	By a Wishing Well
		Wake Up and Live			I've Got a Date with a Dream
		It's Swell of You			Could You Pass in Love?
		Oh, but I'm Happy			This May Be the Night
		I Love You Too Much Muchacha			The All-American Swing
	LOVE AND HISSES	Sweet Someone		LOVE FINDS ANDY HARDY	Meet the Beat of My Heart
		Broadway's Gone Hawaiian			What Do You Know about Love?
		I Wanna Be in Winchell's Column			It Never Rains but What It Pours
		Be a Good Sport		SALLY, IRENE AND MARY	Sweet as a Song
		Lost in Your Eyes			Got My Mind on Music
				JOSETTE	Where in the World?
					In Any Language
					May I Drop a Petal in Your Glass of Wine?
				THANKS FOR EVERYTHING	Thanks for Everything
					You're the World's Fairest
					Three Cheers for Henry Smith
					Puff-A-Puff
				REBECCA OF SUNNYBROOK FARM	An Old Straw Hat
				I'LL GIVE A MILLION	Fond of You
				HOLD THAT CO-ED	Here Am I Doing It
					Hold That Co-ed

1939	ROSE OF WASHINGTON SQUARE	I Never Knew Heaven Could Speak
	THE RAINS CAME	The Rains Came
	TAILSPIN	Are You in the Mood for Mischief?
1940	MOON OVER BURMA	Mexican Magic
	TWO GIRLS ON BROADWAY	Broadway's Still Broadway
1941	FOUR JACKS AND A JILL	You Go Your Way I'm in Good Shape (for the Shape I'm In) Karanina Wherever You Are I Haven't a Thing to Wear Boogie Woogie Conga
1942	THE MAYOR OF 44TH STREET	When There's a Breeze on Lake Louise Heavenly, Isn't It?
	CALL OUT THE MARINES	Beware The Light of My Life Went Out Call Out the Marines Zana Zoranda Hands Across the Border
	THE BIG STREET	Who Knows?
	JOAN OF OZARK	Backwoods Barbecue The Lady at Lockheed
	SING YOUR WORRIES AWAY	Cindy Lou McWilliams It Just Happened to Happen Sing Your Worries Away Sally, My Dear Sally
	MOONLIGHT MASQUERADE	What Am I Doing Here in Your Arms?
	BEYOND THE BLUE HORIZON	A Full Moon and an Empty Heart
	HERE WE GO AGAIN	Delicious Delirium Until I Live Again
1943	HIT THE ICE	I'd Like to Set You to Music I'm Like a Fish Out of Water Happiness Bound The Slap Polka

	IT AIN'T HAY	Glory Be! Old Timer The Sunbeam Serenade
1944	MINSTREL MAN	Remember Me to Carolina Cindy I Don't Care If the World Knows about It Shakin' Hands with the Sun The Bamboo Cane
	GHOST CATCHERS	Blue Candlelight and Red, Red Roses Three Cheers for the Customer Quoth the Raven
1945	THE STORK CLUB	If I Had a Dozen Hearts
	THE DOLLY SISTERS	Powder, Lipstick and Rouge
1947	IT HAPPENED ON FIFTH AVENUE	It's a Wonderful, Wonderful Feeling Speak My Heart! You're Everywhere That's What Christmas Means to Me
1952	THE HALF-BREED	Remember the Girl You Left Behind

You Can't Have Everything (Twentieth Century-Fox, 1937).
Roy Bishop Collection.

Burton Lane

Burton Lane

Burton Lane was the youngest of the songwriters imported by Hollywood when film musicals regained their popularity in 1933. He was born in New York City in 1912 and entered the music profession as a pianist for the Remick Music Corporation when he was just 15 years old. Within three years, Lane's melodies had been introduced to Broadway theatergoers in the revue *Three's a Crowd* and the 1930 editions of *Earl Carroll's Vanities* and *Artists and Models*. After three more stage revues, the 22-year-old composer was hired by Metro-Goldwyn-Mayer to write songs for *Dancing Lady* (1933) starring Joan Crawford and Clark Gable. The picture featured the most durable ballad Lane was ever to write, "Everything I Have Is Yours."

Burton Lane followed his first hit film song with the 1934 successes "Little Did I Dream" from *Bottoms Up*, "Your Head on My Shoulder" from *Kid Millions*, and "Like Me a Little Bit Less" from *Palooka*. In 1935, the United Artists' musical *Folies Bergere* starring Maurice Chevalier featured Lane's "You Took the Words Right Out of My Mouth." The following year, the tunesmith settled down to a five-year contract with Paramount. The first of his compositions to place on "Your Hit Parade" was "Stop, You're Breakin' My Heart" sung by hillbilly Judy Canova in the 1937 release *Artists and Models*. During his employment at Paramount, Lane provided songs for such stars as Bing Crosby, Dorothy Lamour, Gladys Swarthout, Fred MacMurray, Harriet Hilliard, Betty Grable, and Bob Hope. He was represented on the 1938 and 1939 "Hit Parade" surveys by "How'dja Like to Love Me?," "The Lady's in Love with You," and "Says My Heart," which became number one during its twelve-week run on the broadcast.

In the early 1940s, Burton Lane began creating primarily for MGM. He received his first recognition from the Academy of Motion Picture Arts and Sciences when his composition "How About You?" introduced by Judy Garland in *Babes on Broadway*, was nominated as the Best Song of 1941. During World War II, Lane wrote melodies for such MGM successes as *Ship Ahoy* starring Red Skelton and Eleanor Powell, *Panama Hattie* starring Ann Sothern, and *DuBarry Was a Lady* starring Lucille Ball. After the war, Lane returned to Broadway to write the score for the long-run 1947 musical comedy *Finian's Rainbow*.

By the time Burton Lane resumed his career as a motion picture composer, screen musicals were beginning to lose their box office appeal. His 1951 project for MGM proved an exception, and *Royal Wedding* starring Fred Astaire and Jane Powell was an unqualified success. Lane's score for the film included the rousing "How Could You Believe Me When I Said I Loved You When You Know I've Been a Liar All My Life?" and "Too Late Now," which brought the composer his second Academy Award nomination. Burton Lane completed two more musicals for MGM before returning to the stage—*Give a Girl a Break* in 1953 and *Jupiter's Darling* in 1955. In 1970 Lane supplied songs added to the film adaptation of his Broadway musical comedy *On a Clear Day You Can See Forever*.

The Film Songs of Burton Lane

1933	DANCING LADY	Everything I Have Is Yours Let's Go Bavarian		HIDEAWAY GIRL	Dancing into My Heart Two Birdies Up a Tree
	TURN BACK THE CLOCK	Tony's Wife		KING OF GAMBLERS	I'm Feeling High
1934	BOTTOMS UP	Little Did I Dream Turn on the Moon Throwin' My Love Away		WELLS FARGO	Where I Ain't Been Before
				PARTNERS OF THE PLAINS	Moonlight on the Sunset Trail
	KID MILLIONS	Your Head on My Shoulder I Want to Be a Minstrel Man	1938	SPAWN OF THE NORTH	I Wish I Was the Willow I Like Hump-Backed Salmon
	PALOOKA	Like Me a Little Bit Less (Love Me a Little Bit More)		COCOANUT GROVE	Says My Heart Ten Easy Lessons Swami Song
	STRICTLY DYNAMITE	Swing It, Sister Oh Me, Oh My, Oh You		COLLEGE SWING	Moments like This How'dja Like to Love Me? What Did Romeo Say to Juliet?
	THE BAND PLAYS ON	Roll Up the Score			
	COMING OUT PARTY	I Think You're Wonderful			
	LONG LOST FATHER	It Isn't So Much That I Wouldn't		LOVE ON TOAST	I Want a New Romance
1935	FOLIES BERGERE	You Took the Words Right Out of My Mouth	1939	SOME LIKE IT HOT	The Lady's in Love with You
	SHADOW OF A DOUBT	Beyond the Shadow of a Doubt		SHE MARRIED A COP	I'll Remember I Can't Imagine Here's to Love
	HERE COMES THE BAND	You're My Thrill The Army Band I'm Bound for Heaven		ST. LOUIS BLUES	Blue Nightfall Junior The Song in My Heart Is the Rhumba
	RECKLESS	Hear What My Heart Is Saying Trocadero		CAFE SOCIETY	Kiss Me with Your Eyes
	THE PERFECT GENTLEMAN	It's Only Human		FLIGHT AT MIDNIGHT	I Never Thought I'd Fall in Love Again
1936	COLLEGE HOLIDAY	Who's That Knockin' at My Heart? The Sweetheart Waltz	1941	BABES ON BROADWAY	How About You? Babes on Broadway Anything Can Happen in New York Chin Up, Cheerio, Carry On
	EVERY SATURDAY NIGHT	Breathes There a Man			
1937	ARTISTS AND MODELS	Stop, You're Breakin' My Heart Pop Goes the Bubble		DANCING ON A DIME	I Hear Music Manana Dancing on a Dime
	CHAMPAGNE WALTZ	When Is a Kiss Not a Kiss?		LAS VEGAS NIGHTS	I Gotta Ride Mary, Mary, Quite Contrary
	DOUBLE OR NOTHING	Smarty Listen My Children and You Shall Hear		WORLD PREMIERE	Don't Cry Little Cloud
	SWING HIGH, SWING LOW	Swing High, Swing Low			
	HER HUSBAND LIES	No More Tears You Gambled with Love			

163

1942	SHIP AHOY	Poor You
		Last Call for Love
		I'll Take Tallulah
	PANAMA HATTIE	The Son of a Gun That Picks on Uncle Sam
	HER CARDBOARD LOVER	I Dare You
1943	DUBARRY WAS A LADY	Madam, I Love Your Crepe Suzette
		DuBarry Was a Lady
	THOUSANDS CHEER	I Dug a Ditch in Wichita
	PRESENTING LILY MARS	Sweethearts of America
1944	HOLLYWOOD CANTEEN	What Are You Doin' the Rest of Your Life?
		You Can Always Tell a Yank
	RAINBOW ISLAND	Beloved
		What a Day Tomorrow
		We Have So Little Time
		The Boogie Woogie Boogie Man Will Get You If You Don't Watch Out
1945	PILLOW TO POST	Whatcha Say?
1947	THIS TIME FOR KEEPS	I Love to Dance
1951	ROYAL WEDDING	Too Late Now
		Sunday Jumps
		Open Your Eyes
		I Left My Hat in Haiti
		You're All the World to Me
		Ev'ry Night at Seven
		How Could You Believe Me When I Said I Loved You When You Know I've Been a Liar All My Life?
		The Happiest Day of My Life

1953	GIVE A GIRL A BREAK	Ach, Du Lieber Oom-Pah-Pah
		It Happens Ev'ry Time
		Applause, Applause
		In Our United State
		Give a Girl a Break
1955	JUPITER'S DARLING	I Never Trust a Woman
		I Have a Dream
		The Life of an Elephant
		If This Be Slav'ry
		Don't Let This Night Get Away
		Hannibal's Victory March
		Horatio's Narration
1970	ON A CLEAR DAY YOU CAN SEE FOREVER	Love with All the Trimmings
		Go to Sleep, Go to Sleep, Go to Sleep

Ship Ahoy (Metro-Goldwyn-Mayer, 1942).
Collectors Book Store, Hollywood, CA.

Paul Francis Webster

Paul Francis Webster

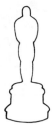

One of the names appearing most frequently on the lists of nominees for the Best Song Oscar is that of Paul Francis Webster. Sixteen songs for which he furnished the lyrics have been nominated since 1943. Webster is another of the many successful popular song writers who was born in New York City. His first jobs as a seaman and a dancing teacher made little use of the formal education he received at Cornell and New York universities. He was 24 years old when the success of his song "Masquerade" started him on a career as a lyricist in 1931. Two years later, his work was heard by Broadway audiences in *Murder at the Vanities*, and he wrote the words for the hit "My Moonlight Madonna." Despite his limited experience as a professional songwriter, he was singled out for a contract with Fox Studios.

The first films to feature the lyrics of Paul Francis Webster were released in 1935: *Under the Pampas Moon* starring Warner Baxter, *Dressed to Thrill* starring Clive Brook, and *Our Little Girl* starring Shirley Temple. Webster moved from Fox to RKO where his assignments consisted almost entirely of creating material for the studio's boy soprano Bobby Breen. Breen sang Webster's songs in *Rainbow on the River* (1936), *Make a Wish* (1937), *Breaking the Ice* (1938), and *Fisherman's Wharf* (1939). The lyricist then worked on such projects as Twentieth Century-Fox's *Tales of Manhattan* (1942), Metro-Goldwyn-Mayer's *Thousands Cheer* (1943), and Producers Releasing Corporation's *Minstrel Man* (1944), which earned Webster an Academy Award nomination for the song "Remember Me to Carolina."

The first of Webster's numbers to make "Your Hit Parade" was "Doctor, Lawyer, Indian Chief" introduced by Betty Hutton in Paramount's *The Stork Club* (1945). His career as a motion picture lyricist went into a decline until 1950 when he began working steadily for MGM. One of the studio's biggest box office attractions was tenor Mario Lanza. Webster reworked Juventino Rosas' instrumental classic "Over the Waves" into "The Loveliest Night of the Year." Lanza sang it in the 1951 musical *The Great Caruso* and it became a "Hit Parade" favorite.

In the early fifties, Paul Francis Webster began collaborating with composer Sammy Fain. Working together, both men achieved their greatest success in Hollywood. Warner Brothers hired the new team to supply the score for its musical *Calamity Jane* starring Doris Day. Their work brought Webster the 1953 Best Song Oscar for his words to "Secret Love." In addition to the award, the number was the first of Webster's inventions to lead "Your Hit Parade." Within two years, Webster had collected his second statuette for the title song "Love Is a Many-Splendored Thing." From 1956 through 1963, the lyricist received nine more Oscar bids for his songs "Thee I Love" (1956), "April Love" (1957), "A Certain Smile" (1958), "A Very Precious Love" (1958), "Green Leaves of Summer" (1960), "The Falcon and the Dove" (1961), "Tender Is the Night" (1962), "Follow Me" (1962), and "So Little Time" (1963). Webster was employed on such spectacular motion pictures as *Giant*, *Raintree County*, *The Alamo*,

El Cid, The Guns of Navarone, Mutiny on the Bounty, and *55 Days at Peking*. A more modest offering, *The Sandpiper* starring Elizabeth Taylor and Richard Burton, brought Webster his third Academy Award for "The Shadow of Your Smile" in 1965. He added words to Maurice Jarre's "Lara's Theme" from the epic *Doctor Zhivago*, and it became one of the most popular songs of 1966—"Somewhere My Love."

At 72, Paul Francis Webster was still active as a motion picture lyricist. His most recent Oscar nominations have been for "A Time to Love" from *An American Dream* (1966), "Strange Are the Ways of Love" from *The Stepmother* (1972), and "A World That Never Was" from *Half a House* (1976).

1935	UNDER THE PAMPAS MOON	Querida Mia
	DRESSED TO THRILL	My One Big Moment My Heart Is a Violin
	OUR LITTLE GIRL	Our Little Girl
1936	RAINBOW ON THE RIVER	Rainbow on the River A Thousand Dreams of You You Only Live Once
1937	MAKE A WISH	Make a Wish Music in My Heart Birch Lake Forever My Campfire Dreams Old Man Rip
	VOGUES OF 1938	Put Your Heart in a Song The Sunny Side of Things Happy as a Lark Telling My Troubles to a Mule Goodbye, My Dreams, Goodbye
1939	FISHERMAN'S WHARF	Blue Italian Waters
1942	SEVEN SWEETHEARTS	You and the Waltz and I
	TALE OF MANHATTAN	Fare-Thee-Well to El Dorado A Journey to Your Lips A Tale of Manhattan
1943	HIT THE ICE	I'd Like to Set You to Music I'm Like a Fish Out of Water Happiness Bound The Slap Polka
	THOUSANDS CHEER	Three Letters in the Mail Box
	PRESENTING LILY MARS	Kulebiaka When I Look at You Is It Really Love (or the Gypsy in Me?)

	IT AIN'T HAY	Glory Be! Old Timer The Sunbeam Serenade
1944	MINSTREL MAN	Remember Me to Carolina Cindy I Don't Care If the World Knows about It Shakin' Hands with the Sun The Bamboo Cane
	GHOST CATCHERS	Blue Candlelight and Red, Red Roses Three Cheers for the Customer Quoth the Raven
1945	THE STORK CLUB	Doctor, Lawyer, Indian Chief If I Had a Dozen Hearts
	JOHNNY ANGEL	Memphis in June
	HOW DO YOU DO?	Boogie Woogie Cindy
1947	IT HAPPENED ON FIFTH AVENUE	You're Everywhere
1950	A LIFE OF HER OWN	A Life of Her Own
1951	THE GREAT CARUSO	The Loveliest Night of the Year
1952	INVITATION	Invitation
	BECAUSE YOU'RE MINE	The Song Angels Sing
1953	CALAMITY JANE	Secret Love The Deadwood Stage The Black Hills of Dakota Keep It under Your Hat A Woman's Touch Higher Than a Hawk I've Got a Hive Full of Honey 'Tis Harry I'm Plannin' to Marry I Can Do without You Just Blew in from the Windy City
	BLOWING WILD	Blowing Wild
	HER MAJESTY O'KEEFE	Emerald Isle

Year	Film	Songs
1954	LUCKY ME	I Speak to the Stars The Blue Bells of Broadway The Supersition Song I Wanna Sing like an Angel Love You Dearly Take a Memo to the Moon
	THE STUDENT PRINCE	Beloved I'll Walk with God Summertime in Heidelberg
	ROSE-MARIE	I Have the Love The Right Place for a Girl Free to Be Free Love and Kisses
	YOUNG AT HEART	There's a Rising Moon Till My Love Comes to Me
1955	LOVE IS A MANY-SPLENDORED THING	Love Is a Many-Splendored Thing
	BATTLE CRY	Honey Babe
	AIN'T MISBEHAVIN'	A Little Love Can Go a Long, Long Way
	SINCERELY YOURS	Sincerely Yours
1956	FRIENDLY PERSUASION	Thee I Love
	ANASTASIA	Anastasia
	GIANT	There's Never Been Anyone Else but You Giant
	HOLLYWOOD OR BUST	Hollywood or Bust A Day in the Country It Looks Like Love Let's Be Friendly The Wild and Woolly West
	THE REVOLT OF MAMIE STOVER	If You Wanna See Mamie Tonight
1957	RAINTREE COUNTY	The Song of Raintree County Never Till Now
	APRIL LOVE	April Love Clover in the Meadow Do It Yourself Give Me a Gentle Girl
	LET'S BE HAPPY	Let's Be Happy One Is a Lonely Number Hold on to Love Man from Idaho I'm Going to Scotland
	A FAREWELL TO ARMS	Love Theme
	MAN ON FIRE	Man on Fire
	BOY ON A DOLPHIN	Boy on a Dolphin
1958	A CERTAIN SMILE	A Certain Smile
	MARJORIE MORNINGSTAR	A Very Precious Love
	THE GIFT OF LOVE	The Gift of Love
	MARDI GRAS	I'll Remember Tonight Mardi Gras March Bourbon Street Blues Stonewall Jackson Bigger Than Texas Loyalty A Fiddle, a Rifle, an Ax and a Bible That Man Could Sell Me the Brooklyn Bridge
	GREEN MANSIONS	Song of Green Mansions
1959	RIO BRAVO	Rio Bravo My Rifle, My Pony and Me
	IMITATION OF LIFE	Imitation of Life
1960	THE ALAMO	The Green Leaves of Summer Ballad of the Alamo Tennessee Babe Here's to the Ladies
	CIMARRON	Cimarron

1961	EL CID	The Falcon and the Dove	
	THE GUNS OF NAVARONE	Guns of Navarone	
	RETURN TO PEYTON PLACE	Season of Love	
1962	TENDER IS THE NIGHT	Tender Is the Night	
	MUTINY ON THE BOUNTY	Follow Me	
1963	55 DAYS AT PEKING	So Little Time	
1964	THE SEVENTH DAWN	The Seventh Dawn	
	36 HOURS	A Heart Must Learn to Cry	
1965	THE SANDPIPER	The Shadow of Your Smile	
	JOY IN THE MORNING	Joy in the Morning	
	SYLVIA	Sylvia	

1966	AN AMERICAN DREAM	A Time for Love
	MADE IN PARIS	Paris Lullaby
1967	THREE BITES OF AN APPLE	In the Garden—Under the Tree The Swindle The Serpent Mr. Thrumm's Chase
1969	HEAVEN WITH A GUN	A Lonely Place
1972	THE STEPMOTHER	Strange Are the Ways of Love
1975	MR. SYCAMORE	Time Goes By
1976	HALF A HOUSE	A World That Never Was

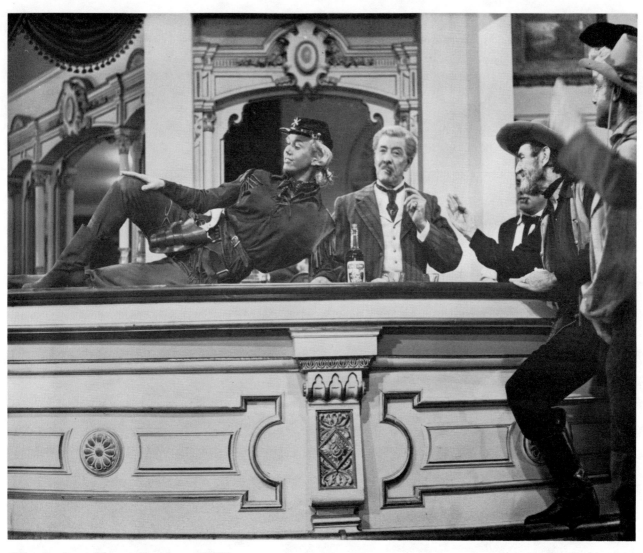

Calamity Jane (Warner Brothers, 1953).
Collectors Book Store, Hollywood, CA.

Harold Arlen

Harold Arlen had a solid reputation as a popular music composer at the time he accepted his first Hollywood offer in 1934. The first five years of his songwriting career had produced such hits as "Between the Devil and the Deep Blue Sea," "I Love a Parade," "I Gotta Right to Sing the Blues," "It's Only a Paper Moon," "I've Got the World on a String," and "Let's Take a Walk Around the Block." Arlen was born in Buffalo, New York, in 1905. He left high school before graduation and began playing the piano in silent movie theatres. He then formed his own jazz group for which he functioned as arranger, pianist, and vocalist. He achieved his first encouragement as a composer when his melody "Get Happy" was accepted for the 1930 Broadway production *9:15 Revue*. The song's success convinced Arlen to change his vocation from performing to songwriting. His work was heard in quick succession in six more stage musicals and in floor shows staged at Harlem's Cotton Club. His contribution to four editions of the Cotton Club Revue included his 1933 classic "Stormy Weather." After completing the score for the musical comedy *Life Begins at 8:40*, Arlen boarded the train that was to take him to Hollywood.

The studio at which Harold Arlen began his career in motion pictures was a minor one. Columbia was known primarily for low budget films of less than top quality. Arlen's project was *Let's Fall in Love* starring Ann Sothern, who had been known on the Broadway stage as Harriet Lake. No one connected with the film expected the tremendous reaction of the public to the film's title song, which became one of the biggest hits of 1934.

Arlen moved his base from Columbia to Warner Brothers, where he wrote melodies introduced by Dick Powell in *Gold Diggers of 1937* and Al Jolson in *The Singing Kid*. He then began twenty years as a free-lance composer moving from one major studio to another. Arlen worked on United Artists' *Strike Me Pink*, Paramount's *Artists and Models*, RKO's *Love Affair*, and Metro-Goldwyn-Mayer's *The Wizard of Oz*. His score for *The Wizard of Oz* included "Over the Rainbow," a song that the studio was less than enthusiastic about. Despite the opinions of the MGM moguls, "Over the Rainbow" was voted as the Best Song of 1939. It also rose to the top of "Your Hit Parade." The next year, the composer returned to Warner Brothers, which was preparing a dramatic musical concerning the lives of professional musicians. Arlen's melody "Blues in the Night" proved so outstanding that the studio gave the film the same title.

After winning the 1939 Oscar, Arlen had seven more songs nominated for Hollywood's highest honor during the next eight years: "Blues in the Night," "That Old Black Magic," "Happiness Is a Thing Called Joe," "My

175

Shining Hour," "Ac-cent-tchu-ate the Positive," "Now I Know," and "For Every Man There's a Woman." "Blues in the Night" and "Ac-cent-tchu-ate the Positive" each led "Your Hit Parade."

Arlen's success as a motion picture songwriter continued into the 1950s. He created the scores for two of the most important screen musicals of 1954: *A Star Is Born*, in which Judy Garland returned to the cameras for the first time in five years; and *The Country Girl*, which won Grace Kelly the Academy Award for Best Performance by an Actress. Arlen was also nominated for his ninth Oscar that year for "The Man That Got Away" from *A Star Is Born*. The last two films on which he worked were *Gay Purree* (1962) and *I Could Go on Singing* (1963). Both pictures reunited him with Judy Garland who had become permanently associated with the Arlen classics "Over the Rainbow" and "The Man That Got Away."

During his years as a motion picture composer, Harold Arlen returned to Broadway periodically for the productions *Hooray for What*, *Bloomer Girl*, *St. Louis Woman*, *House of Flowers*, *Jamaica*, and *Saratoga*. None of the songs from their scores ever achieved the popularity of the dozens of hits he created for the screen.

The entire nation honored the talent of Harold Arlen in a television salute on the occasion of his sixty-eighth birthday in 1973. His contemporary, composer George Gershwin, referred to Arlen as "the most original of us all."

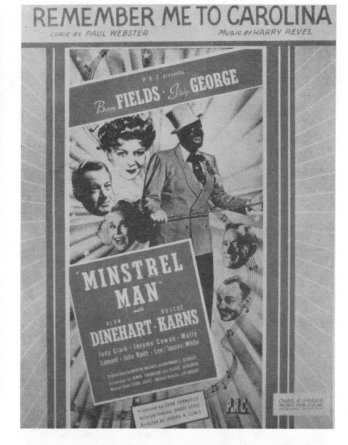

1934	LET'S FALL IN LOVE	Let's Fall in Love Love Is Love Anywhere This Is Only the Beginning Breakfast Ball	AT THE CIRCUS — Lydia, the Tattooed Lady Two Blind Loves Step Up and Take a Bow Swingali

1934   LET'S FALL IN LOVE   Let's Fall in Love
Love Is Love Anywhere
This Is Only the Beginning
Breakfast Ball

         AT THE CIRCUS   Lydia, the Tattooed Lady
Two Blind Loves
Step Up and Take a Bow
Swingali

1936   GOLD DIGGERS OF 1937   Speaking of the Weather
Let's Put Our Heads
   Together
Life Insurance Song
Hush Ma Mouth

         LOVE AFFAIR   Sing, My Heart

1941   BLUES IN THE NIGHT   Blues in the Night
This Time the Dream's on
   Me
Says Who? Says You, Says
   I!
Hang on to Your Lids,
   Kids

         THE SINGING KID   You're the Cure for What
   Ails Me
I Love to Sing-a
My How This Country Has
   Changed
Save Me, Sister
Here's Looking at You

1942   STAR SPANGLED
RHYTHM   That Old Black Magic
Hit the Road to Dreamland
Old Glory
A Sweater a Sarong and a
   Peek-a-boo Bang
I'm Doing It for Defense
Sharp as a Tack
On the Swing Shift
He Loved Me Till the
   All-Clear Came

         STAGE STRUCK   Fancy Meeting You
In Your Own Quiet Way
You're Kinda Grandish
The New Parade

         STRIKE ME PINK   The Lady Dances
First You Have Me High
Calabash Pipe
If I Feel This Way
   Tomorrow Then It's Love

         CAIRO   Buds Won't Bud

         RIO RITA   Long Before You Came
   Along

         CAPTAINS OF THE
CLOUDS   Captains of the Clouds

1937   ARTISTS AND MODELS   Public Melody Number
   One

1939   THE WIZARD OF OZ   Over the Rainbow
Ding, Dong, the Witch Is
   Dead
If I Only Had a Brain
We're Off to See the
   Wizard
In the Merry Old Land of
   Oz
Munchkinland
The Jitterbug

1943   CABIN IN THE SKY   Happiness Is a Thing
   Called Joe
Life's Full o' Consequence
Li'l Black Sheep
Ain't It de Truth

         THE SKY'S THE LIMIT   My Shining Hour
One for My Baby
I've Got a Lot in Common
   with You
Harvey, the Victory Garden
   Man

         THEY GOT ME COVERED   Palsy Walsy

1944	HERE COMES THE WAVES	Ac-cent-tchu-ate the Positive Let's Take the Long Way Home I Promise You There's a Fellow Waitin' in Poughkeepsie My Mamma Thinks I'm a Star Here Come the Waves	

1944 HERE COMES THE WAVES
- Ac-cent-tchu-ate the Positive
- Let's Take the Long Way Home
- I Promise You
- There's a Fellow Waitin' in Poughkeepsie
- My Mamma Thinks I'm a Star
- Here Come the Waves

UP IN ARMS
- Now I Know
- Tess's Torch Song
- All Out for Freedom

KISMET
- Willow in the Wind
- Tell Me, Tell Me Evening Star

1945 OUT OF THIS WORLD
- Out of This World
- June Comes Around Every Year

1947 CASBAH
- For Every Man There's a Woman
- It Was Written in the Stars
- Horray for Love
- What's Good about Goodbye?
- The Monkey Sat in the Cocoanut Tree

1950 THE PETTY GIRL
- Fancy Free
- Ah Loves Ya
- Calypso Song
- The Petty Girl

MY BLUE HEAVEN
- Live Hard, Work Hard, Love Hard
- The Friendly Islands
- It's Deductible
- Halloween
- Don't Rock the Boat, Dear
- What a Man
- I Love a New Yorker
- Cosmo Cosmetics

1951 MR. IMPERIUM
- Andiamo
- Let Me Look at You
- My Love and My Mule

1953 DOWN AMONG THE SHELTERING PALMS
- I'm a Ruler of a South Sea Island
- The Opposite Sex
- Who Will It Be When the Time Comes?
- What Make de Diff'rence?

THE FARMER TAKES A WIFE
- Today I Love Everybody
- With the Sun Warm upon Me
- On the Erie Canal
- We're Doin' It for the Natives in Jamaica
- When I Close My Door
- Somethin' Real Special
- We're in Business
- Can You Spell Schenectady?

1954 A STAR IS BORN
- The Man That Got Away
- It's a New World
- Here's What I'm Here For
- Gotta Have Me Go with You
- Someone at Last
- Lose That Long Face

	THE COUNTRY GIRL	It's Mine, It's Yours		Take My Hand, Paree
		Dissertation on a State of Bliss		Paris Is a Lonely Town
				Bubbles
		The Search Is Through		Roses Red, Violets Blue
		The Land around Us		The Horse Won't Talk
1962	GAY PURR-EE	Mewsette	1963 I COULD GO ON SINGING	I Could Go on Singing
		Little Drops of Rain		
		The Money Cat		
		Portraits of Mewsette		

The Wizard of Oz (Metro-Goldwyn-Mayer, 1939).
Bill Chapman Collection.

Courtesy of Betty Kern Miller

Jerome Kern

The Broadway theater was a long time recovering from the shock of Jerome Kern's defection to Hollywood in 1934. No other composer had been as instrumental in developing musical comedy into an art form. For over fifteen years, Kern had worked to transform musicals from a collection of songs, dances, and comedy routines into integrated productions in which each of those elements furthered the progress of a show's story. Kern's name was synonymous with the best in American musical comedy.

Jerome Kern was born into an upper middle-class New York family in 1885. He was 17 when his first song was accepted for the 1902 production *The Silver Slipper*. He studied at Heidelberg University and returned to the United States with a Master of Music degree in 1905. For the next eight years, his melodies were featured in over two dozen Broadway musicals. His big break came when his song "They Didn't Believe Me" became the hit of the 1914 offering *The Girl from Utah*. The next year, he composed the score for the first Princess Theatre show *Nobody Home*. It was followed by three more musicals for the group: *Very Good, Eddie, Oh, Boy!* and *Oh, Lady! Lady!* All the productions were acclaimed for their intelligence and credibility. Kern's greatest achievement came in 1927 with *Show Boat*, which was hailed as the theater's most artistic musical accomplishment. He further enhanced his reputation with *The Cat and the Fiddle*, *Music in the Air*, and *Roberta*. The creator of such unforgettable melodies as "Look for the Silver Lining," "Ol' Man River," "Only Make

Believe," "Why Was I Born?," "She Didn't Say Yes," "The Song Is You," and "Smoke Gets in Your Eyes" then announced his signing of a contract with RKO film studios, and the Broadway theater lost its most distinguished living composer.

Forty-nine-year-old Jerome Kern began his Hollywood career by creating a new song for the screen version of *Roberta*—"Lovely to Look At." His composition rose to "Your Hit Parade's" top spot and won Kern an Oscar nomination for the Best Song of 1935. The next year, RKO released *Swing Time* starring Fred Astaire and Ginger Rogers. The film introduced two more classics: "A Fine Romance" and "The Way You Look Tonight," which earned Kern his first Academy Award. It had taken the veteran musical comedy composer just two films to disprove the notion that Broadway show tunes were superior to other types of popular music. The medium for which popular songs were created was of no consequence. Kern's next outstanding score was written for Paramount's 1937 road show presentation *High, Wide and Handsome* in which Irene Dunne, Randolph Scott, and Dorothy Lamour appeared. His 1938 film *Joy of Living* produced another of his songs that made "Your Hit Parade"—"You Couldn't Be Cuter."

Jerome Kern was presented with his second Oscar for "The Last Time I Saw Paris." The composer felt the honor unwarranted since his song had not been written especially for the screen, but had been interpolated into Metro-Goldwyn-Mayer's 1941 release *Lady Be Good*.

His dissatisfaction caused the Academy to alter its rules so that future Best Song candidates were limited to those created for specific motion pictures.

Like Irving Berlin, Kern's reputation enabled him to pick and choose his film assignments, and any studio lucky enough to acquire Kern's services was assured of obtaining an unmatchable score. Columbia engaged the composer for its 1942 musical *You Were Never Lovelier* starring Fred Astaire and Rita Hayworth. The film earned Kern another Academy Award bid for his melody "Dearly Beloved." He then provided Columbia with the classic "Long Ago (and Far Away)" for *Cover Girl* and wrote the hit "More and More" for Universal's *Can't Help Singing*. The two compositions competed for the Best Song Oscar in 1944 and 1945. Sixty-year-old Kern suffered a fatal stroke in 1945. Both Hollywood and Broadway were reminded of their loss when Twentieth Century-Fox released *Centennial Summer* the next year. Jerome Kern's last score brought the celebrated composer a posthumous Academy Award nomination for his melody "All through the Day." When *Roberta* was remade as *Lovely to Look At* in 1952, the score included three additional Kern compositions with new lyrics by Dorothy Fields.

The Film Songs of Jerome Kern

1935	ROBERTA	Lovely to Look At ✓
		I Won't Dance ✓
	I DREAM TOO MUCH	I Dream Too Much
		Jockey on the Carousel
		I Got Love
		I'm the Echo
	SWEET ADELINE	We Were So Young
	RECKLESS	Reckless
1936	SWING TIME	The Way You Look Tonight ✓
		A Fine Romance ✓
		Pick Yourself Up
		Bojangles of Harlem
		The Waltz in Swingtime
		Never Gonna Dance
	SHOW BOAT	I Still Suits Me
		I Have the Room Above
1937	HIGH, WIDE AND HANDSOME	The Folks Who Live on the Hill
		Can I Forget You?
		High, Wide and Handsome
		Will You Marry Me Tomorrow, Maria?
		Allegheny Al
		The Things I Want
	WHEN YOU'RE IN LOVE	Our Song
		The Whistling Song
1938	JOY OF LIVING	You Couldn't Be Cuter ✓
		Just Let Me Look at You
		What's Good about Goodnight?
		A Heavenly Party

1940	ONE NIGHT IN THE TROPICS	Remind Me
		You and Your Kiss
		Farendola
		Simple Philosophy
		Back in My Shell
1941	LADY BE GOOD	The Last Time I Saw Paris
1942	YOU WERE NEVER LOVELIER	Dearly Beloved
		I'm Old-Fashioned
		You Were Never Lovelier
		Wedding in the Spring
		On the Beam
		The "Shorty George"
1943	SONG OF RUSSIA	And Russia Is Her Name
1944	COVER GIRL	Long Ago (and Far Away)
		Sure Thing
		Make Way for Tomorrow
		Put Me to the Test
		Cover Girl
		The Show Must Go On
		Who's Complaining?
	CAN'T HELP SINGING	More and More
		Any Moment Now
		Can't Help Singing
		Californi-ay
		Elbow Room
		Swing Your Sweetheart 'round the Fire
1946	CENTENNIAL SUMMER	All through the Day
		In Love in Vain
		Up with the Lark
		Two Hearts Are Better Than One
		The Right Romance
		Cinderella Sue
1952	LOVELY TO LOOK AT	Opening Night
		Lafayette
		The Most Exciting Night

186

Can't Help Singing (Universal, 1944).
Academy of Motion Picture Arts and Sciences Library,
Beverly Hills, CA.

Courtesy of Regan Burke

Johnny Burke

Most of Hollywood's great songwriters worked for several studios. Johnny Burke was the only one who spent his entire career under contract to one organization. Burke was born in Antioch, California, in 1908. His family moved to Chicago where his father operated a construction firm. Burke was educated at the University of Wisconsin and played the piano in the college orchestra. When he graduated, he was hired by Irving Berlin's music publishing company as a staff pianist. Burke was 25 years old when he wrote the words for one of the biggest hit songs of 1933—"Annie Doesn't Live Here Anymore." He continued to show promise as a lyricist with such numbers as "Beat of My Heart," "It's Dark on Observatory Hill," "My Very Good Friend, the Milkman," and "You're So Darn Charming." The consistent popularity of his songs landed him a Hollywood contract in the mid-thirties.

Johnny Burke's first outstanding work for the screen was the title number for the film *Pennies from Heaven* which was nominated as the Best Song of 1936. Bing Crosby's recording of the song was one of the year's top sellers. Of the forty-one films on which Johnny Burke worked, twenty-five starred Crosby. These musicals introduced seventeen songs that made "Your Hit Parade" including the leaders "Pennies from Heaven," "I've Got a Pocketful of Dreams," "Only Forever," "Moonlight Becomes You," and "Sunday, Monday or Always." Burke supplied the lyrics for six of the "Road" pictures in which Crosby co-starred with Bob Hope and Dorothy Lamour.

Johnny Burke's second song to earn an Oscar nomination was "Only Forever" written for the 1940 release *Rhythm on the River*. Four years later, his lyrics to "Swinging on a Star," introduced by Crosby in *Going My Way*, won the lyricist Hollywood's highest award. Burke was in the running again the next year for "Aren't You Glad You're You?" from *Bells of St. Mary's*. Burke's association with Paramount and Bing Crosby continued into the 1950's with the productions *Riding High, Mr. Music, Road to Bali*, and *Little Boy Lost*. The last film on which Burke worked was the studio's remake of *The Vagabond King* released in 1956. Johnny Burke died eight years later at the age of 55.

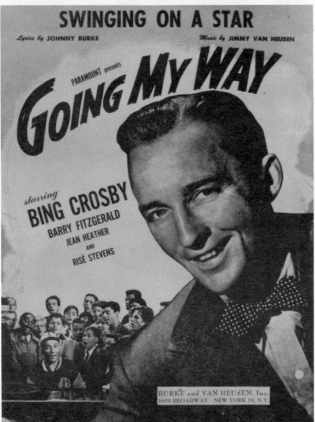

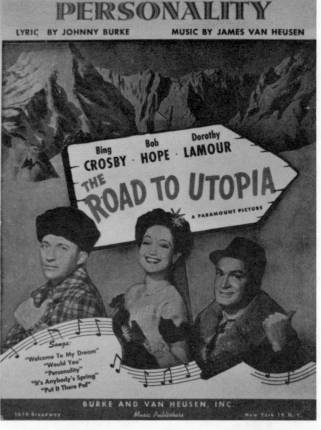

The Film Songs of Johnny Burke

1930	LET'S GO PLACES	Boop Boop a Doopa Doo Trot
1936	PENNIES FROM HEAVEN	Pennies from Heaven ✓
		One, Two, Button Your Shoe
		So Do I
		Let's Call a Heart a Heart
		The Skeleton in the Closet
		Now I've Got Some Dreaming to Do
		What This Country Needs
	GO WEST, YOUNG MAN	I Was Saying to the Moon
		A Typical Tropical Night
		Go West, Young Man
1937	DOUBLE OR NOTHING	The Moon Got in My Eyes
		It's the Natural Thing to Do
		All You Want to Do Is Dance
		Double or Nothing
	MIDNIGHT MADONNA	Love Didn't Know Any Better
1938	SING YOU SINNERS	I've Got a Pocketful of Dreams
		Don't Let That Moon Get Away
		Laugh and Call It Love
		Where Is Central Park?
	DOCTOR RHYTHM	On the Sentimental Side
		My Heart Is Taking Lessons
		This Is My Night to Dream
		Doctor Rhythm
		Only a Gypsy Knows
		P.S. 43
		Trumpet Player's Lament
1939	THAT'S RIGHT—YOU'RE WRONG	Scatterbrain ✓
	THE STAR MAKER	An Apple for the Teacher
		Go Fly a Kite
		A Man and His Dream
		Still the Bluebird Sings
	EAST SIDE OF HEAVEN	East Side of Heaven
		Sing a Song of Sunbeams
		Hang Your Heart on a Hickory Limb
		That Sly Old Gentleman from Featherbed Lane

1940	RHYTHM ON THE RIVER	Only Forever
		That's for Me
		When the Moon Comes Over Madison Square
		Ain't It a Shame about Mame?
		Rhythm on the River
		What Would Shakespeare Have Said?
	ROAD TO SINGAPORE	Too Romantic
		The Moon and the Willow Tree
		Sweet Potato Piper
		Kaigoon
		Captain Custard
	IF I HAD MY WAY	I Haven't Time to Be a Millionaire
		April Played the Fiddle
		Meet the Sun Half-way
		The Pessimistic Character (with the Crabapple Face)
	LOVE THY NEIGHBOR	Do You Know Why?
		Isn't That Just Like Love?
		Dearest, Darest I?
1941	PLAYMATES	Humpty Dumpty Heart
		How Long Did I Dream?
		Romeo Smith and Juliet Jones
		Que Chica
		Thank Your Lucky Stars and Stripes
	ROAD TO ZANZIBAR	It's Always You
		Birds of a Feather
		You're Dangerous
		You Lucky People You
		African Etude
1942	ROAD TO MOROCCO	Moonlight Becomes You ✓
		Road to Morocco
		Ain't Got a Dime to My Name
		Constantly
		Aladdin's Daughter
	MY FAVORITE SPY	Got the Moon in My Pocket
		Just Plain Lonesome

Lady in the Dark (Paramount, 1943).
Larry Edmunds Book Shop, Hollywood, CA.

1943	DIXIE	Sunday, Monday or ✓		AND THE ANGELS SING ↘	It Could Happen to You
		Always			And His Rocking Horse Ran
		If You Please			Away
		She's from Missouri			The First One Hundred
		Miss Jemima Walks By			Years
		Kinda Peculiar Brown			How Does Your Garden
		A Horse That Knows the			Grow?
		Way Back Home			Knockin' on Your Own
					Front Door
1944	GOING MY WAY	Swinging on a Star			Bluebirds in My Belfry
		Going My Way			My Heart's Wrapped Up in
		The Day after Forever			Gingham
					When Stanislaus Got
	LADY IN THE DARK	Suddenly It's Spring ✓			Married

	BELLE OF THE YUKON	Like Someone in Love Sleigh Ride in July Every Girl Is Different Belle of the Yukon	

1945	THE BELLS OF ST. MARY'S	Aren't You Glad You're You?
	ROAD TO UTOPIA	Personality Put It There, Pal Welcome to My Dream It's Anybody's Spring Goodtime Charlie Would You?
	THE GREAT JOHN L	A Friend of Yours A Perfect Gentleman
	DUFFY'S TAVERN	The Hard Way
1946	CROSS MY HEART	That Little Dream Got Nowhere Love Is the Darndest Thing How Do You Do It? Does Baby Feel All Right? It Hasn't Been Chilly in Chile
	MY HEART GOES CRAZY	So Would I My Heart Goes Crazy The 'amstead Way Anyway the Wind Blows Hyde Park on a Sunday You Can't Keep a Good Dreamer Down
1947	WELCOME STRANGER	As Long as I'm Dreaming My Heart Is a Hobo Country Style Smile Right Back at the Sun Smack in the Middle of Maine
	ROAD TO RIO	But Beautiful You Don't Have to Know the Language For What? Apalachicola, Fla. Experience
	VARIETY GIRL	Harmony
	MAGIC TOWN	My Book of Memory
1948	THE EMPEROR WALTZ	Get Yourself a Phonograph Friendly Mountains The Kiss in Your Eyes The Emperor Waltz

	MYSTERY IN MEXICO	Something in Common At the Psychological Moment I Could Get Along with You Rolling in Rainbows
1949	TOP O' THE MORNING	You're in Love with Someone Top o' the Morning
	A CONNECTICUT YANKEE IN KING ARTHUR'S COURT	Once and for Always When Is Sometime? If You Stub Your Toe on the Moon Busy Doing Nothing Twixt Myself and Me
1950	RIDING HIGH	Sunshine Cake Someplace on Anywhere Road The Horse Told Me (We've Got) A Sure Thing
	MR. MUSIC	And You'll Be Home Life Is So Peculiar High on the List Accidents Will Happy Wouldn't It Be Funny? Once More the Blue and White Milady Wasn't I There? Mr. Music
1952	ROAD TO BALI	To See You Moonflowers Chicago Style Hoot Mon Merry-Go-Run-Around
1953	LITTLE BOY LOST	The Magic Window Cela M'est Egal A Propos de Rien
1956	THE VAGABOND KING	A Harp, a Fiddle and a Flute One, Two, Three, Pause Bon Jour This Same Heart Viva la You Comparisons Watch Out for the Devil

Ira Gershwin

Ira Gershwin

Ira Gershwin was the first popular song writer in history to win the Pulitzer Prize for Drama. The award was given for his work on the 1931 Broadway musical comedy *Of Thee I Sing*. Gershwin was the third of Broadway's big name songwriters to carve a niche for himself in Hollywood, following the path already taken by Irving Berlin and Jerome Kern.

Ira Gershwin was born in New York City in 1896. He began his professional career in 1918 using the pen name of Arthur Francis. Many of his early songs were written in collaboration with his younger brother George who attracted international attention with the piano conerto "Rhapsody in Blue," which he composed in 1924. That same year, the Gershwin brothers began working primarily as a team and provided Broadway with such smash musicals as *Lady, Be Good!*, *Oh, Kay!*, *Funny Face*, *Strike Up the Band*, *Girl Crazy*, and *Of Thee I Sing*. These productions introduced such outstanding Ira Gershwin lyrics as "Fascinatin' Rhythm," "Someone to Watch Over Me," " 'S Wonderful," "I've Got a Crush on You," "Embraceable You," "I Got Rhythm," and "Love Is Sweeping the Country." The Gershwins traveled to Hollywood in 1931 to write the score for the Fox musical *Delicious* starring Janet Gaynor and Charles Farrell, but neither man was ready to trade live theater for celluloid. They returned to New York where they created three more

stage musicals including the 1935 folk opera *Porgy and Bess*. When none of the productions matched the success of their earlier Broadway efforts, George and Ira Gershwin accepted an offer from RKO Studios as full-time motion picture songwriters.

In 1937, the Gershwin brothers completed three film scores that equaled any ever written for the screen. *Shall We Dance*, *A Damsel in Distress*, and *Goldwyn Follies* introduced fourteen compositions that became national favorites. The songs "They Can't Take That Away from Me," "Let's Call the Whole Thing Off," "Nice Work If You Can Get It," and "Love Walked In" all made "Your Hit Parade" with the last number capturing the top spot. "They Can't Take That Away from Me" was nominated for the Academy Award.

George Gershwin was stricken with a brain tumor and died suddenly in 1937. Ira resumed his career in 1941 as lyricist for the Broadway production *Lady in the Dark*. He began accepting film offers again in 1943 with RKO's *The North Star*. The following year, he was employed at Columbia on one of the most successful musicals of World War II—*Cover Girl* starring Rita Hayworth and Gene Kelly. Its score included the "Hit Parade" leader "Long Ago (and Far Away)" which brought Ira Gershwin his second Oscar nomination. In 1945, the lyricist worked on Twentieth Century-Fox's unusual musical *Where Do We Go from Here?* in which most of the film's story was told in song with dialogue held to a minimum. The innovation proved too radical for most moviegoers. The score for Fox's *The Shocking Miss Pilgrim* (1947), starring Betty Grable, consisted of unpublished George Gershwin melodies with lyrics added by Ira. When MGM reunited dancing stars Ginger Rogers and Fred Astaire for *The Barkleys of Broadway*—the team's first film together in ten years—Ira Gershwin wrote the words for several new songs. But the number from the picture that attracted the most comment was the Gershwin's "They Can't Take That Away from Me," which Rogers and Astaire had introduced in *Shall We Dance* twelve years earlier.

The last two projects on which Gershwin worked before his retirement at the age of 58 were Paramount's *The Country Girl* starring Bing Crosby and Warner Brothers' *A Star Is Born* starring Judy Garland. "The Man That Got Away" from *A Star Is Born* was nominated as the Best Song of 1954. Ira Gershwin came out of retirement briefly in 1964 when he wrote lyrics for three more of his brother's unpublished compositions. The songs were heard in the film *Kiss Me, Stupid*.

1931	DELICIOUS	Blah, Blah, Blah Delishious Somebody from Somewhere Katinkitschka	1945	WHERE DO WE GO FROM HERE?

1931 DELICIOUS — Blah, Blah, Blah / Delishious / Somebody from Somewhere / Katinkitschka

1932 GIRL CRAZY — You've Got What Gets Me

1937 SHALL WE DANCE — They Can't Take That Away from Me / Let's Call the Whole Thing Off / I've Got Beginner's Luck / They All Laughed / Slap That Bass / Shall We Dance? / Wake Up, Brother, and Dance

A DAMSEL IN DISTRESS — Nice Work If You Can Get It / A Foggy Day / Things Are Looking Up / I Can't Be Bothered Now / Stiff Upper Lip / The Jolly Tar and the Milkmaid

1938 THE GOLDWYN FOLLIES — Love Walked In / Our Love Is Here to Stay / I Was Doing All Right / Spring Again / I Love to Rhyme / I'm Not Complaining

1943 THE NORTH STAR — No Village Like Mine / Song of the Guerrillas

1944 COVER GIRL — Long Ago (and Far Away) / Sure Thing / Cover Girl / Make Way for Tomorrow / Put Me to the Test / The Show Must Go On / Who's Complaining?

1945 WHERE DO WE GO FROM HERE? — All at Once / If Love Remains / Song of the Rhineland / It Happened to Happen to Me / The Nina, the Pinta, the Santa Maria

1947 THE SHOCKING MISS PILGRIM — Back Bay Polka / Changing My Tune / For You, For Me, Forevermore / Aren't You Kinda Glad We Did? / But Not in Boston / Stand Up and Fight / One, Two, Three / Sweet Packard / Waltz Me No Waltzes Sitting Down / Waltzing Is Better Sitting Down

1949 THE BARKLEYS OF BROADWAY — Shoes with Wings On / My One and Only Highland Fling / You'd Be Hard to Replace / Swing Trot / Weekend in the Country / Manhattan Downbeat

1953 GIVE A GIRL A BREAK — Ach, Du Lieber, Oom-Pah-Pah / Applause, Applause / It Happens Ev'ry Time / Give a Girl a Break / In Our United State

1954 A STAR IS BORN — The Man That Got Away / Gotta Have Me Go with You / Lose That Long Face / It's a New World / Here's What I'm Here For / Someone at Last

THE COUNTRY GIRL — It's Mine, It's Yours / Dissertation on a State of Bliss / The Search Is Through / The Land around Us

1964 KISS ME, STUPID — Sophia / I'm a Poached Egg / All the Livelong Day

A Star Is Born (Warner Brothers, 1954).
Collectors Book Store, Hollywood, CA.

Courtesy of Lynn Loesser

Frank Loesser

Frank Loesser

The only songwriter to arrive in Hollywood as a lyricist and leave as a composer was Frank Loesser. He was born in New York City in 1910, and dropped out of college when he was 16. While trying to establish himself as a lyric writer, he took jobs as an office boy, a process server, and a roving reporter. His first published song, "In Love with a Memory of You," resulted in a contract with RKO in the early thirties. When none of his efforts reached the screen, he became a night-club entertainer singing in clubs on New York's Fifty-Second Street. He continued writing and sold material to vaudeville and radio performers. His lyrics were featured in the 1936 stage revue *The Illustrator's Show* and their excellence led to his second contract with a film studio.

Frank Loesser's return trip to Hollywood bore fruit. His lyrics were heard by movie fans in the 1937 releases *Blossoms on Broadway, Fight for Your Lady,* and *Vogues of 1938.* The next year, the broadcasts of "Your Hit Parade" included Loesser's "I Fall in Love with You Every Day," "How'dja Like to Love Me?," "Small Fry," "Two Sleepy People," "Heart and Soul," and the number one song "Says My Heart." The numbers were all introduced in screen musicals produced by Paramount, where Loesser worked for four years. The lyricist provided the studio with songs for such popular attractions as Jack Benny's *Man about Town* and *Buck Benny Rides Again*; Dorothy Lamour's *St. Louis Blues, Moon over Burma, Typhoon,* and *Aloma of the South Seas*; Bob Hope's *Some Like It Hot, Caught in the Draft,* and *Kiss the Boys Goodbye,* starring Mary Martin; and the full-length cartoon *Mr. Bug Goes to Town.* His songs "I Don't Want to Walk without You"

from *Sweater Girl* and "Jingle, Jangle, Jingle" from *The Forest Rangers* both led "Your Hit Parade."

When the United States entered World War II, Frank Loesser served as a Private First Class in the Army's Special Services Division. While supplying sketches and songs for all-soldier revues, he wrote his own music for "Praise the Lord and Pass the Ammunition." The number sold over two million records and a million copies of sheet music.

Loesser returned to civilian life in 1946. His first two Oscar bids had been for the words only to "Dolores" (1941) and "They're Either Too Young or Too Old" (1943); his next two nominations were for both the words and music for "I Wish I Didn't Love You So," introduced by Betty Hutton in *Perils of Pauline* (1947), and "Baby, It's Cold Outside," which Esther Williams and Ricardo Montalban performed in *Neptune's Daughter* (1949). His fourth nomination proved to be a winner, and Loesser collected the Oscar for "Baby, It's Cold Outside."

The year before winning his Academy Award, Frank Loesser created the score for the Broadway hit *Where's Charley?* He followed it with the even more successful musical comedy *Guys and Dolls* in 1950. In 1952, he worked on his last original screen musical, *Hans Christian Andersen* starring Danny Kaye. Its score included "Thumbelina," which brought Loesser another Best Song nomination. The composer-lyricist reached the zenith of his career when he was awarded the Pulitzer Prize for Drama for his 1961 Broadway production *How to Succeed in Business without Really Trying.* Frank Loesser died in 1969 at the age of 59.

1937	THE HURRICANE	Moon of Mana Koora	
	VOGUES OF 1938	Lovely One	
	BLOSSOMS ON BROADWAY	No Ring on Her Finger You Can't Tell a Man by His Hat	
	FIGHT FOR YOUR LADY	Blame It on the Danube	
1938	COCOANUT GROVE	Says My Heart Ten Easy Lessons	
	COLLEGE SWING	I Fall in Love with You Every Day You're a Natural Moments like This How'dja Like to Love Me? What a Rhumba Does to Romance The Old School Bell What Did Romeo Say to Juliet? College Swing	
	SING YOU SINNERS	Small Fry	
	THANKS FOR THE MEMORY	Two Sleepy People	
	SPAWN OF THE NORTH	I Wish I Was the Willow I Like Hump-Backed Salmon	
	A SONG IS BORN	Heart and Soul	
	FRESHMAN YEAR	Chasin' You Around	
	MEN WITH WINGS	Men with Wings	
	STOLEN HEAVEN	The Boys in the Band	
1939	MAN ABOUT TOWN	Strange Enchantment That Sentimental Sandwich Man about Town Fidgety Joe	
	ST. LOUIS BLUES	I Go for That Blue Nightfall Junior The Song in My Heart Is the Rhumba	
	DESTRY RIDES AGAIN	The Boys in the Back Room Little Joe, the Wrangler You've Got That Look	

HAWAIIAN NIGHTS	Hey, Good Lookin' Hawaii Sang Me to Sleep I Found My Love Then I Wrote the Minuet in G	✓
THE GRACIE ALLEN MURDER CASE	Snug as a Bug in a Rug	
SOME LIKE IT HOT	The Lady's in Love with You Some Like It Hot	
CAFE SOCIETY	Kiss Me with Your Eyes Park Avenue Gimp	
HERITAGE OF THE DESERT	Here's a Heart	
INVITATION TO HAPPINESS	Invitation to Happiness	
ISLAND OF LOST MEN	Music on the Shore	
ZAZA	Hello, My Darling Forget Me Zaza	

1940	BUCK BENNY RIDES AGAIN	Say It My! My! Drums in the Night My Kind of Country
	JOHNNY APOLLO	Dancing for Nickels and Dimes Your Kiss
	MOON OVER BURMA	Moon over Burma Mexican Magic
	SEVEN SINNERS	I've Been in Love Before I've Fallen Overboard The Man's in the Navy
	TYPHOON	Palms of Paradise
	A NIGHT AT EARL CARROLL'S	Li'l Boy Love I Wanna Make with the Happy Times
	THE FARMER'S DAUGHTER	Jungle Jingle
	NORTH WEST MOUNTED POLICE	Does the Moon Shine through the Tall Pine?

	THE QUARTERBACK	Out with Your Chest
	SEVENTEEN	Seventeen
	YOUTH WILL BE SERVED	Hot Catfish and Corn Dodgers
1941	LAS VEGAS NIGHTS	Dolores I Gotta Ride Mary, Mary, Quite Contrary
	KISS THE BOYS GOODBYE	Sand in My Shoes Kiss the Boys Goodbye I'll Never Let a Day Pass By That's How I Got My Start Find Yourself a Melody
	MR. BUG GOES TO TOWN	We're the Couple in the Castle Boy, Oh Boy! I'll Dance at Your Wedding Katy-Did, Katy-Didn't

	GLAMOUR BOY	The Magic of Magnolias Love Is Such an Old-Fashioned Thing
	ALOMA OF THE SOUTH SEAS	The White Blossoms of Tah-ni
	SAILORS ON LEAVE	Since You
	DANCING ON A DIME	I Hear Music Manana Dancing on a Dime Lovable Sort of Person
	HOLD BACK THE DAWN	My Boy, My Boy
	WORLD PREMIERE	Don't Cry Little Cloud
	CAUGHT IN THE DRAFT	Love Me as I am
	SIS HOPKINS	Cracker Barrel County If You're in Love Look at You, Look at Me Well! Well! That Ain't Hay
1942	PRIORITIES ON PARADE	You're in Love with Someone Else

SEVEN DAYS' LEAVE	Can't Get Out of This Mood
	A Touch of Texas
	I Get the Neck of the
	   Chicken
	Softhearted
	Please, Won't You Leave
	   My Girl Alone?
	You Speak My Language
	Puerto Rico
		TORTILLA FLAT	Oh, How I Love a Wedding
			Ai-Paisano

		1943 THANK YOUR LUCKY
		   STARS
			They're Either Too Young
			   or Too Old
			How Sweet You Are
			The Dreamer
			I'm Ridin' for a Fall
			Good Night, Good
			   Neighbor
			Love Isn't Born
			Ice Cold Katy
			Thank Your Lucky Stars
			We're Staying Home
			   Tonight
			I'm Goin' North
			That's What You Jolly Well
			   Get

SWEATER GIRL	I Don't Want to Walk without You I Said No What Gives Out Now? Sweater Girl		
THE FOREST RANGERS	Jingle, Jangle, Jingle		
TRUE TO THE ARMY	Need I Speak? Jitterbug's Lullaby Spangles on My Tights In the Army Wacky for Khaki	HAPPY GO LUCKY	Let's Get Lost Murder, He Says Happy Go Lucky Sing a Tropical Song Fuddy Duddy Watchmaker
BEYOND THE BLUE HORIZON	Pagan Lullaby	TORNADO	There Goes My Dream
REAP THE WILD WIND	Sea Chanty		
THIS GUN FOR HIRE	Now You See It I've Got You		

1944	CHRISTMAS HOLIDAY	Spring Will Be a Little Late This Year
	SEE HERE, PRIVATE HARGROVE	In My Arms
1945	DUFFY'S TAVERN	Leave Us Face It (We're in Love)
1947	THE PERILS OF PAULINE	The Sewing Machine I Wish I Didn't Love You So Rumble, Rumble, Rumble Poppa, Don't Preach to Me
	VARIETY GIRL	Tallahassee He Can Waltz Your Heart Calling Mine I Must Have Been Madly in Love I Want My Money Back Impossible Things The French
1949	NEPTUNE'S DAUGHTER	Baby, It's Cold Outside My Heart Beats Faster I Love Those Men

	RED, HOT AND BLUE	Now That I Need You That's Loyalty Hamlet I Wake Up in the Morning Feeling Fine
	ROSEANNA McCOY	Roseanna
1950	LET'S DANCE	I Can't Stop Thinking about Him Why Fight the Feeling? Oh, Them Dudes Tunnel of Love Jack and the Beanstalk The Hyacinth
1952	HANS CHRISTIAN ANDERSEN	Thumbelina Wonderful Copenhagen No Two People The Inch Worm Anywhere I Wander
1955	GUYS AND DOLLS	A Woman in Love Adelaide Pet Me Poppa

The Perils of Pauline (Paramount, 1947).
Collectors Book Store, Hollywood, CA.

Courtesy of Mrs. Virginia Monaco and Mrs. George L.
Romano

Jimmie Monaco

The Italian parents of Jimmie Monaco brought their 6-year-old son to the United States in 1891. He got his start in show business playing the piano in saloons in Chicago and New York when ragtime music was the national craze. Monaco's career as a songwriter caught fire in 1912 when his melodies "Row, Row, Row" and "You Made Me Love You" sold millions of copies of sheet music. They were followed by the hits "I Miss You Most of All" and "What Do You Want to Make Those Eyes at Me For?" and songs featured in such Broadway productions as *Robinson Crusoe Jr.*, *Afgar*, the 1921 edition of *The Ziegfeld Follies*, and *Harry Delmar's Revels* staged in 1927. The year *Delmar's Revels* opened, audiences at New York's Warner Theatre heard Al Jolson sing from the screen for the first time. One of the numbers Jolson performed in *The Jazz Singer* was "Dirty Hands, Dirty Face" with music by Jimmie Monaco.

Monaco's first tour of duty in Hollywood began in 1930 when his songs were heard in the "talkies" *The Golden Calf* starring Sue Carol, *Let's Go Places* with Lola Lane, and *The Dancers* featuring Lois Moran. The most popular of his melodies of this period was "Crazy People," which the comedy team of Burns and Allen adopted as their theme song. The number was featured in Paramount's *The Big Broadcast* in 1932. The next few years of Monaco's career were spent conducting his own dance orchestra.

Jimmie Monaco was in his early fifties when he returned to the Paramount payroll in 1936. Bing Crosby had been the studio's top musical star for four years during which most of his songs had been written by the teams of Leo Robin and Ralph Rainger and Mack Gordon and Harry Revel. Since Paramount made as many as fifteen musicals a year, the studio was pressed to keep its performers supplied with quality material. Jimmie Monaco was assigned to work with lyricist Johnny Burke on the scores of Crosby's *Doctor Rhythm* and *Sing You Sinners*. The songs they created rivaled the best of Robin and Rainger and Gordon and Revel and included the favorites "My Heart Is Taking Lessons," "On the Sentimental Side," and "I've Got a Pocketful of Dreams," which became the number one song on "Your Hit Parade." Monaco worked on five more Crosby vehicles during the next two years: *The Star Maker*, *East Side of Heaven*, *If I Had My Way*, *Rhythm on the River*, and *Road to Singapore*, which began the popular series starring Crosby with Bob Hope and Dorothy Lamour. Monaco's melodies from these musicals included "An Apple for the Teacher," "A Man and His Dream," "Go Fly a Kite," "Too Romantic," and another "Hit Parade" leader, "Only Forever," which earned the composer his first Academy Award nomination.

Monaco lost his ace lyricist when Johnny Burke began collaborating with Paramount's newest staff composer James Van Heusen. Working with other partners at United Artists and Twentieth Century-Fox, Monaco contributed to the scores for six more productions from 1941 through 1945. He received Oscar nominations for his songs "We Mustn't Say Goodbye" from *Stage Door Canteen* (1943), "I'm Making Believe" from *Sweet and Lowdown* (1944), and "I Can't Begin to Tell You" introduced by Betty Grable in *The Dolly Sisters* (1945). Sixty-year-old "Ragtime Jimmie" Monaco died of a heart ailment the year "I Can't Begin to Tell You" became the number one song from coast to coast.

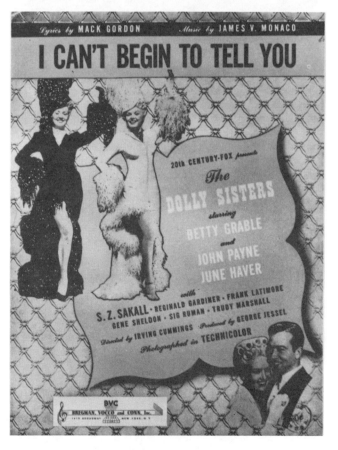

1930	THE GOLDEN CALF	Can I Help It?
		I'm Tellin' the World about You
		Maybe, Someday
		Modernistic
	LET'S GO PLACES	Let's Go Places
	ON THE LEVEL	Good Intentions
	THE DANCERS	Love Has Passed Me By
1931	HOLY TERROR	Lonesome Lover
	ROAD TO SINGAPORE	Hand in Hand
1932	THE BIG BROADCAST	Crazy People
1938	DOCTOR RHYTHM	My Heart Is Taking Lessons
		On the Sentimental Side
		This Is My Night to Dream
		Doctor Rhythm
		Only a Gypsy Knows
		P.S. 43
		Trumpet Player's Lament
	SING YOU SINNERS	I've Got a Pocketful of Dreams
		Laugh and Call It Love
		Don't Let That Moon Get Away
		Where Is Central Park?
1939	THE STAR MAKER	An Apple for the Teacher
		A Man and His Dream
		Go Fly a Kite
		Still the Bluebird Sings
	EAST SIDE OF HEAVEN	Hang Your Heart on a Hickory Limb
		East Side of Heaven
		Sing a Song of Sunbeams
		That Sly Old Gentleman from Featherbed Lane
1940	ROAD TO SINGAPORE	Too Romantic
		Sweet Potato Piper
		Kaigoon
	IF I HAD MY WAY	Meet the Sun Half-way
		April Played the Fiddle
		I Haven't Time to Be a Millionaire
		The Pessimistic Character (with the Crabapple Face)
	RHYTHM ON THE RIVER	Only Forever
		That's for Me
		When the Moon Comes over Madison Square
		Ain't It a Shame about Mame?
		Rhythm on the River
		What Would Shakespeare Have Said?
1941	WEEKEND IN HAVANA	Romance and Rhumba
1943	STAGE DOOR CANTEEN	We Mustn't Say Goodbye
		American Boy
		Don't Worry Island
		Quick Sands
		A Rookie and His Rhythm
		Sleep, Baby, Sleep
		We'll Meet in the Funniest Places
		You're Pretty Terrific Yourself
		She's a Bombshell from Brooklyn
1944	SWEET AND LOWDOWN	I'm Making Believe
		Hey, Bub, Let's Have a Ball
		Ten Days with Baby
		One Chord in Two Flats
		Tsk, Tsk, That's Love
		Chug-Chug, Choo-Choo, Chug
	PIN-UP GIRL	Once Too Often
		Time Alone Will Tell
		You're My Little Pin-Up Girl
		Yankee Doodle Hayride
		The Story of the Very Merry Widow
		Don't Carry Tales Out of School
		Red Robins, Bob Whites and Bluebirds
	IRISH EYES ARE SMILING	Bessie in a Bustle
		I Don't Want a Million Dollars
1945	THE DOLLY SISTERS	I Can't Begin to Tell You
		Don't Be Too Old-Fashioned (Old-Fashioned Girl)

212

The Dolly Sisters (Twentieth Century-Fox, 1945).
Collectors Book Store, Hollywood, CA.

From the Bill Chapman Collection

Jule Styne

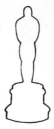

Most of Hollywood's great songwriters worked in the legitimate theater before turning their attention to motion pictures. Jule Styne reversed the usual process by spending almost ten years writing for films before embarking on one of the most successful Broadway careers in contemporary history. Styne was born in London in 1905. He was a child prodigy whose performances at the piano amazed concert audiences. When he was 9 years old, his parents brought him to the United States, where he received an extensive musical education. Instead of pursuing the classics, Styne worked as a pianist with jazz bands in Chicago. When he was 22 years old, he collaborated on the song "Sunday" published in 1927. In the early 1930s, Styne formed his own dance orchestra and supported himself as a performing musician until he landed a contract as composer, arranger, and vocal coach at Twentieth Century-Fox. His first assignments were comedies, released in 1938, featuring Joan Davis and the Ritz Brothers.

As the forties began, Jule Styne moved from Fox to one of Hollywood's lesser-known film factories, Republic. The studio's stock in trade was low-budget westerns, and Styne wrote songs for such Gene Autry and Roy Rogers oaters as *Melody Ranch, Back in the Saddle, Bad Man of Deadwood,* and *Sheriff of Tombstone.* The highlights of Styne's tenure at Republic were Academy Award nominations for his melodies "Who Am I?" and "Change of Heart," written for the

studio's musical series *The Hit Parade.* The composer's fortunes brightened in 1942 when "I've Heard That Song Before" from *Youth on Parade* and "I Don't Want to Walk Without You" from *Sweater Girl* both made the number one spot on "Your Hit Parade." "I've Heard That Song Before" earned Styne another Oscar bid. In 1944, he worked at Universal where he created his fourth Academy Award contender "I'll Walk Alone."

His years of work on such program fillers as *Henry Aldrich Swings It, Here Comes Elmer,* and *Rosie, the Riveter* were ended by the mid-forties, and Jule Styne's talent was in demand at every major studio on the West Coast. In 1945, his melodies "I Fall in Love Too Easily" from Metro-Goldwyn-Mayer's *Anchors Aweigh* and "Anywhere" from Columbia's *Tonight and Every Night* competed against each other for the Best Song award. The stars with whom he was associated included Frank Sinatra, Gene Kelly, Rita Hayworth, Betty Hutton, Danny Kaye, Dennis Morgan, and Jack Carson. Doris Day introduced Styne's Oscar candidates "It's Magic" in *Romance on the High Seas* (1948) and "It's a Great Feeling" (1949) in the film of the same title. After more than fifteen years of writing for films, Styne won the Academy Award for his 1954 title song "Three Coins in the Fountain."

Hollywood bestowed its highest honor on Jule Styne after he had received accolades for his long-run Broadway musicals *High Button Shoes* in 1947 and *Gentlemen*

Prefer Blondes in 1949. Styne found his career in the legitimate theater more challenging than the film assignments offered during the decline of screen musicals. Although his stage hits *Bells Are Ringing*, *Gypsy* and *Funny Girl* were filmed in 1960, 1962 and 1968, the only original motion picture musical on which Jule Styne worked during the sixties was Shirley MacLaine's 1964 vehicle *What a Way to Go!* The composer who left Hollywood to make good on Broadway received his tenth Academy Award nomination for his title song added to the film adaptation of *Funny Girl*.

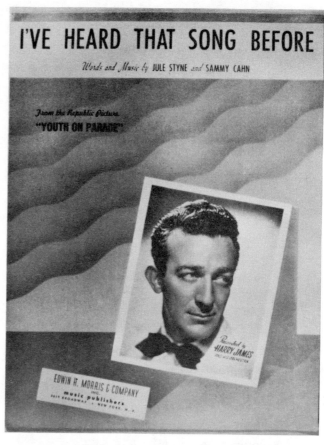

1938	HOLD THAT CO-ED	Limpy Dimp		MELODY AND MOONLIGHT	Rooftop Serenade Tahiti Honey Top o' the Mornin' I Close My Eyes Melody and Moonlight
	STRAIGHT, PLACE AND SHOW	International Cowboys			
	KENTUCKY MOONSHINE	Kentucky Opera	1941	SAILORS ON LEAVE	Since You
1939	PACK UP YOUR TROUBLES	Who'll Buy My Flowers?		ANGELS WITH BROKEN WINGS	Bye-Lo Baby Has to Be In Buenos Aires Three Little Wishes Where Do We Dream from Here?
	STOP, LOOK AND LOVE	Let's Start Where We Left Off			
1940	THE HIT PARADE OF 1941	Who Am I? In the Cool of the Evening Make Yourself at Home Swing Low, Sweet Rhythm		PUDDIN' HEAD	Hey, Junior You're Telling I Manhattan Holiday Puddin' Head
	SING, DANCE, PLENTY HOT	I'm Just a Weakie Too Toy When a Fella's Got a Girl Tequila What Fools These Mortals Be		ROOKIES ON PARADE	Rookies on Parade
				DOCTORS DON'T TELL	Lilly and Billy Take My Heart (for Instance)
	GIRL FROM HAVANA	Querida The Girl from Havana		ICE-CAPADES	Forever and Ever
	THE HOUSE ACROSS THE BAY	Chula Chihuahua		RAGS TO RICHES	The Call of Love Never, Never, Never
	SLIGHTLY HONORABLE	Cupid's After Me		BACK IN THE SADDLE	Swingin' Sam, the Cowboy Man Where the River Meets the Range
	MELODY RANCH	Torpedo Joe What Are Cowboys Made Of? Rodeo Rose Stake Your Dreams on Melody Ranch		BAD MAN OF DEADWOOD	Joe O'Grady
				WEST OF THE CIMARRON	Wa-Wa-Watermelon

	SIS HOPKINS	Cracker Barrel County
		If You're in Love
		Look at You, Look at Me
		Well! Well!
		That Ain't Hay
	DOWN MEXICO WAY	Down Mexico Way
	IN OLD CHEYENNE	Bonita
	JESSE JAMES AT BAY	Just for You
	NEVADA CITY	Lonely Hills
		Prairie Serenade
	PALS OF THE PECOS	Don Pedro Pistachio
	RIDIN' ON A RAINBOW	Hunky Dory
		Sing a Song of Laughter
		What's Your Favorite Holiday?
		I'm the One Who's Lonely
	SHERIFF OF TOMBSTONE	Ridin' on a Rocky Road
		Ya Should'a Seen Pete
	THE SINGING HILL	Tumble Down Shack in Havana
1942	YOUTH ON PARADE	I've Heard That Song Before
		You're So Good to Me
	PRIORITIES ON PARADE	Conchita Marquita Lolita Pepita Rosita Juanita Lopez
		You're in Love with Someone Else
		I'd Love to Know You Better
		Here Comes Katrinka
		Cooperate with Your Air Raid Warden
	SWEATER GIRL	I Don't Want to Walk without You
		I Said No
		What Gives Out Now?
		Sweater Girl

	SLEEPYTIME GAL	I Don't Want Anybody at All
		Barrelhouse Bessie from Basin Street
		When the Cat's Away
	BEYOND THE BLUE HORIZON	Pagan Lullaby
	ICE-CAPADES REVUE	The Guy with the Polka-Dotted Tie
	JOHNNY DOUGHBOY	Baby's a Big Girl Now
		All Done, All Through
		It Takes a Guy like I
		Victory Caravan
	THE OLD HOMESTEAD	Dig, Dig, Dig for Victory
	THE POWERS GIRL	Three Dreams
		Out of This World
		The Lady Who Didn't Believe in Love
		Partners
		We're Looking for the Big Bad Wolf
1943	LARCENY WITH MUSIC	For the Want of You
	LET'S FACE IT	Plain Jane Doe
		Who Did? I Did, Yes I Did
	HIT PARADE OF 1943	Change of Heart
		Do These Old Eyes Deceive Me?
		Harlem Sandman
		That's How to Write a Song
		Who Took Me Home Last Night?
		Tahm-Boom-Bah

SALUTE FOR THREE	Don't Worry	
	I'd Do It for You	
	Wha' D'ya Do When It Rains?	
	My Wife's a WAC	
	Left-Right	
THUMBS UP	From Here on In	
	Love Is a Corny Thing	
	Who Are the British?	
HENRY ALDRICH SWINGS IT	Ding-Dong—Sing a Song	
SHANTYTOWN	On the Corner of Sunshine and Main	
THE HEAT'S ON	Thinkin' about the Wabash	
1944 FOLLOW THE BOYS	I'll Walk Alone	
	A Better Day Is Coming	
CAROLINA BLUES	There Goes That Song Again	
	Poor Little Rhode Island	
	You Make Me Dream Too Much	
	Thanks a Lot	
	Mister Beebe	
JAM SESSION	Vict'ry Polka	

STEP LIVELY	Come Out, Come Out, Wherever You Are	
	And Then You Kissed Me	
	Where Does Love Begin?	
	Why Must There Be an Op'ning Song?	
	Ask the Madam	
	As Long as There's Music	
	Some Other Time	
KNICKERBOCKER HOLIDAY	One More Smile	
	Love Has Made This Such a Lovely Day	
JANIE	Keep Your Powder Dry	
1945 ANCHORS AWEIGH	I Fall in Love Too Easily	
	The Charm of You	
	I Begged Her	
	What Makes the Sunset?	
	We Hate to Leave	
TONIGHT AND EVERY NIGHT	Anywhere	
	Cry and You Cry Alone	
	The Heart of a City	
	Tonight and Every Night	
	What Does an English Girl Think of a Yank?	
	The Boy I Left Behind	
	You Excite Me	
THE STORK CLUB	Love Me	
1946 SWEETHEART OF SIGMA CHI	Five Minutes More	
TARS AND SPARS	I'm Glad I Waited for You	
	Kiss Me Hello	
	Love Is a Merry-Go-Round	
	He's a Hero	
	I Love Eggs	
	After the War, Baby	
	I Have a Love in Every Port	
	When I Get to Town	
	Don't Call on Me	
	I Always Meant to Tell You	

CINDERELLA JONES	When the One You Love Simply Won't Love Back If You're Waitin', I'm Waitin', Too Cinderella Jones You Never Know Where You're Goin' Till You Get There Our Theme	

1948 ROMANCE ON THE HIGH SEAS
It's Magic
It's You or No One
Put 'em in a Box
The Tourist Trade
I'm in Love
Run, Run, Run
Two Lovers Met in the Night

EARL CARROLL'S SKETCH BOOK
I've Never Forgotten The Lady with a Mop
Oh, Henry!
What Makes You Beautiful, Beautiful?
I Was Silly, I Was Head-strong, I Was Impetuous
We Met Over a Bottle of Vino
Salvo

TWO GUYS FROM TEXAS
Every Day I Love You
I Don't Care If It Rains All Night
Hankerin'
There's Music in the Land
I Never Met a Texan
I Wanna Be a Cowboy in the Movies
At the Rodeo

THE KID FROM BROOKLYN
I Love an Old-Fashioned Song
You're the Cause of It All
Hey, What's Your Name?
Josie
Sunflower Song
Pavlova

MIRACLE OF THE BELLS   Ever Homeward

SONS OF ADVENTURE   If It's Love

1947 IT HAPPENED IN BROOKLYN
Time after Time
I Believe
It's the Same Old Dream
The Brooklyn Bridge
Whose Baby Are You?
The Song's Gotta Come from the Heart

1949 IT'S A GREAT FEELING
It's a Great Feeling
Fiddle Dee Dee
Blame My Absent-Minded Heart
At the Cafe Rendezvous
There's Nothin' Rougher Than Love
Give Me a Song with a Beautiful Melody
That Was a Big Fat Lie

LADIES' MAN
What Am I Gonna Do About You?
I Gotta Gal I Love
Away Out West
I'm as Ready as I'll Ever Be

1950	THE WEST POINT STORY	Ten Thousand Four Hundred and Thirty-Two Sheep By the Kissing Rock You Love Me Military Polka Long Before I Knew You The Corps It Could Only Happen in Brooklyn
1951	MEET ME AFTER THE SHOW	Let Go of My Heart Meet Me after the Show Betting on a Man It's a Hot Night in Alaska No Talent Joe I Feel Like Dancing
	TWO TICKETS TO BROADWAY	The Closer You Are Are You Just a Beautiful Dream? Baby, You'll Never Be Sorry Let the Worry Bird Worry for You Big Chief Hole-in-the-Ground Pelican Falls High It Began in Yucatan New York

	DOUBLE DYNAMITE	It's Only Money Kisses and Tears
1952	MACAO	You Kill Me Talk to Me Tomorrow Ocean Breeze
1953	THREE COINS IN THE FOUNTAIN	Three Coins in the Fountain
	LIVING IT UP	Money Burns a Hole in My Pocket That's What I Like
1954	CHANGE OF HEART	If It's Love
1955	HOW TO BE VERY, VERY POPULAR	How to Be Very, Very Popular
	MY SISTER EILEEN	Give Me a Band and My Baby There's Nothin' like Love It's Bigger Than You and Me
	THE SEVEN YEAR ITCH	The Seven Year Itch
1960	BELLS ARE RINGING	Better Than a Dream
1963	ALL THE WAY HOME	All the Way Home
1964	WHAT A WAY TO GO!	Get Acquainted Happy Houseboat
1968	FUNNY GIRL	Funny Girl The Swan Roller Skate Rag

Two Tickets to Broadway (RKO, 1951).
Collectors Book Store, Hollywood, CA.

James Van Heusen

James Van Heusen

James Van Heusen is one of the three composers of popular songs to have been in the winner's circle at the annual Oscar sweepstakes on four occasions. Van Heusen was born in Syracuse, New York, in 1913. He entered show business playing the piano and singing on a local radio station when he was in high school. While working as a staff pianist for a music publisher in 1934, he succeeded in selling his song "There's a House in Harlem for Sale." Within five years, eleven numbers with music by Van Heusen had been featured on "Your Hit Parade," including "Darn That Dream," "Heaven Can Wait," and "Imagination" in First Place.

In 1940, the 27-year-old tunesmith was placed under contract by Paramount where he succeeded Ralph Rainger, Harry Revel, and Jimmie Monaco as Bing Crosby's chief composer. Van Heusen and lyricist Johnny Burke supplied songs for sixteen Crosby musicals, which featured such hits as "It's Always You" (*Road to Zanzibar*, 1941), "Moonlight Becomes You" (*Road to Morocco*, 1942), "Sunday, Monday or Always" (*Dixie*, 1943), "Personality" (*Road to Utopia*, 1945), and "But Beautiful" (*Road to Rio*, 1947). Crosby also introduced Van Heusen's first Oscar winner, "Swinging on a Star," in *Going My Way* in 1944 and his second Academy Award candidate "Aren't You Glad You're

You?" in *Bells of St. Mary's* the next year. Other personalities with whom Van Heusen was associated were Kay Kyser, whose orchestra performed "Humpty Dumpty Heart" in *Playmates*, Betty Hutton who sang "It Could Happen to You" in *And the Angels Sing*, and Dinah Shore who introduced "Sleigh Ride in July" in *Belle of the Yukon*.

When James Van Heusen's partnership with Johnny Burke was dissolved in the mid-fifties, the composer began working with lyricist Sammy Cahn. During the fourteen years of the their collaboration, eleven of Van Heusen's compositions were nominated for Oscars. His three additional Academy Award winners were "All the Way" (1957), "High Hopes" (1959), and "Call Me Irresponsible" (1963). The thin line between winners and losers is apparent by the excellence of Van Heusen's also-rans: "(Love Is) The Tender Trap," "To Love and Be Loved," "The Second Time Around," "Pocketful of Miracles," "My Kind of Town," "Where Love Has Gone," "Thoroughly Modern Millie," and "Star!"

Van Heusen was one of the few Hollywood songwriters whose success continued throughout the decade of the sixties when he worked on almost two dozen film assignments.

The Film Songs of James Van Heusen

1940 LOVE THY NEIGHBOR — Do You Know Why? / Isn't That Just like Love? / Dearest, Darest I?

1941 PLAYMATES — Humpty Dumpty Heart / How Long Did I Dream? / Romeo Smith and Juliet Jones / Que Chica / Thank Your Lucky Stars and Stripes

ROAD TO ZANZIBAR — It's Always You / Birds of a Feather / You're Dangerous / You Lucky People You / Road to Zanzibar / African Etude

1942 ROAD TO MOROCCO — Moonlight Becomes You / Constantly / Road to Morocco / Ain't Got a Dime to My Name / Aladdin's Daughter

MY FAVORITE SPY — Got the Moon in My Pocket / Just Plain Lonesome

1943 DIXIE — Sunday, Monday or Always / If You Please / She's from Missouri / Miss Jemima Walks By / Kinda Peculiar Brown / A Horse That Knows the Way Back Home

1944 GOING MY WAY — Swinging on a Star / The Day after Forever / Going My Way

LADY IN THE DARK — Suddenly It's Spring

AND THE ANGELS SING — It Could Happen to You / And His Rocking Horse Ran Away / The First One Hundred Years / How Does Your Garden Grow? / Knockin' on Your Own Front Door / Bluebirds in My Belfry / My Heart's Wrapped Up in Gingham / When Stanislaus Got Married

BELLE OF THE YUKON — Like Someone in Love / Sleigh Ride in July / Every Girl Is Different / Belle of the Yukon

1945 THE BELLS OF ST. MARY'S — Aren't You Glad You're You?

ROAD TO UTOPIA — Personality / Welcome to My Dream / It's Anybody's Spring / Put It There, Pal / Goodtime Charlie / Would You?

DUFFY'S TAVERN — The Hard Way

THE GREAT JOHN L — A Friend of Yours / A Perfect Gentleman

227

1946	CROSS MY HEART	That Little Dream Got Nowhere
		Love Is the Darndest Thing
		How Do You Do It?
		Does Baby Feel All Right?
		It Hasn't Been Chilly in Chile
	MY HEART GOES CRAZY	So Would I
		My Heart Goes Crazy
		The 'ampstead Way
		Anyway the Wind Blows
		Hyde Park on a Sunday
		You Can't Keep a Good Dreamer Down
1947	WELCOME STRANGER	As Long as I'm Dreaming
		Smile Right Back at the Sun
		Country Style
		My Heart Is a Hobo
		Smack in the Middle of Maine
	ROAD TO RIO	But Beautiful
		You Don't Have to Know the Language
		Apalachicola, Fla.
		For What?
		Experience
	VARIETY GIRL	Harmony
	MAGIC TOWN	My Book of Memory

1948	THE EMPEROR WALTZ	Get Yourself a Phonograph
	MYSTERY IN MEXICO	Something in Common
		At the Psychological Moment
		I Could Get Along with You
		Rolling in Rainbows
1949	TOP O' THE MORNING	You're in Love with Someone
		Top o' the Morning
	A CONNECTICUT YANKEE IN KING ARTHUR'S COURT	Once and for Always
		When Is Sometime?
		If You Stub Your Toe on the Moon
		Busy Doing Nothing
		Twixt Myself and Me
1950	MR. MUSIC	Life Is So Peculiar
		High on the List
		And You'll Be Home
		Accidents Will Happen
		Wouldn't It Be Funny?
		Once More the Blue and White
		Milady
		Wasn't I There?
		Mr. Music
	RIDING HIGH	Sunshine Cake
		Someplace on Anywhere Road
		The Horse Told Me
		(We've Got) A Sure Thing
1952	ROAD TO BALI	Merry-Go-Run-Around
		Moonflowers
		To See You
		Chicago Style
		Hoot Mon

1953	LITTLE BOY LOST	A Propos de Rien
		The Magic Window
		Cela M'est Egal
1954	YOUNG AT HEART	You, My Love
1955	THE TENDER TRAP	(Love Is) The Tender Trap
	NOT AS A STRANGER	Not as a Stranger
1956	ANYTHING GOES	A Second Hand Turban and a Crystal Ball
		Ya Gotta Give the People Hoke
		You Can Bounce Right Back
	PARDNERS	Pardners
		Buckskin Beauty
		Wind, the Wind
		Me 'n' You 'n' the Moon
		The Test of Time
1957	THE JOKER IS WILD	All the Way
1958	SOME CAME RUNNING	To Love and Be Loved
	INDISCREET	Indiscreet
	PARIS HOLIDAY	Life Is for Lovin'
		Love Won't Let You Get Away
		Nothing in Common

1959	A HOLE IN THE HEAD	High Hopes
		All My Tomorrows
	THEY CAME TO CORDURA	They Came to Cordura
	SAY ONE FOR ME	Say One for Me
		You Can't Love 'em All
		Chico's Choo-Choo
		The Secret of Christmas
		The Night That Rock 'n' Roll Died (Almost)
		You're Starting to Get to Me
		I Couldn't Care Less
		The Girl Most Likely to Succeed
	CAREER	(Love Is a) Career
	THIS EARTH IS MINE	This Earth Is Mine
	JOURNEY TO THE CENTER OF THE EARTH	My Love Is Like a Red, Red Rose
		Twice as Tall
		The Faithful Heart
		Come Spring
		I'm Never Alone
	NIGHT OF THE QUARTER MOON	Night of the Quarter Moon
	HOLIDAY FOR LOVERS	Holiday for Lovers
1960	HIGH TIME	The Second Time Around
		Nobody's Perfect
		Showmanship
		Go! Go! Go!
	WAKE ME WHEN IT'S OVER	Wake Me When It's Over

	WHO WAS THAT LADY?	Who Was That Lady?	
	THE WORLD OF SUZIE WONG	Suzie Wong	
	OCEAN'S 11	Ain't That a Kick in the Head?	
		Ee-o Eleven	
	LET'S MAKE LOVE	Incurably Romantic	
		Hey, You with the Crazy Eyes	
		Specialization	
		Let's Make Love	
1961	POCKETFUL OF MIRACLES	Pocketful of Miracles	
1962	ROAD TO HONG KONG	Warmer Than a Whisper	
		Teamwork	
		Let's Not Be Sensible	
		The Road to Hong Kong	
		The Only Way to Travel	
	BOYS' NIGHT OUT	The Boys' Night Out	
		Cathy	
1963	PAPA'S DELICATE CONDITION	Call Me Irresponsible	
	COME BLOW YOUR HORN	Come Blow Your Horn	
		The Look of Love	
	UNDER THE YUM YUM TREE	Under the Yum Yum Tree	
	4 FOR TEXAS	Four for Texas	
	MY SIX LOVES	It's a Darn Good Thing	
		My Six Loves	
	JOHNNY COOL	The Ballad of Johnny Cool	

1964	ROBIN AND THE 7 HOODS	My Kind of Town	
		Style	
		I Like to Lead When I Dance	
		All for One and One for All	
		Mister Booze	
		Charlotte Couldn't Charleston	
		Any Man Who Loves His Mother	
		Don't Be a Do-Badder	
		Bang-Bang	
		Give Praise, Give Praise, Give Praise	
	WHERE LOVE HAS GONE	Where Love Has Gone	
	THE PLEASURE SEEKERS	Everything Makes Music When You're in Love	
		Costa del Sol	
	HONEYMOON HOTEL	Honeymoon Hotel	
1965	THE SECOND BEST SECRET AGENT IN THE WHOLE WIDE WORLD	The Second Best Secret Agent in the Whole Wide World	
1967	THOROUGHLY MODERN MILLIE	Thoroughly Modern Millie	
		The Tapioca	
1968	STAR!	Star!	
1969	THE GREAT BANK ROBBERY	Rainbow Rider	
		Heaven Helps Him Who Helps Himself	

Road to Bali (Paramount, 1952).
Academy of Motion Picture Arts and Sciences Library,
Beverly Hills, CA.

Sammy Cahn

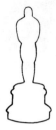

The age-old question as to which is more important to a song—its music or its lyrics—seems to be answered by the work of Sammy Cahn. Over a period of thirty-three years, twenty-six numbers with lyrics by Cahn have been nominated as the Best Song of the year. No writer of melodies has ever been accorded such recognition. The lyricist's Oscar contending songs have been written with well-known composers Jule Styne and James Van Heusen as well as with lesser-known tunesmiths Nicholas Brodszky, Victor Young, Alfred Newman, and George Barrie. In four separate years, Cahn had two numbers competing for the same Academy Award.

Sammy Cahn was born in New York City in 1913. While trying to gain a foothold as a songwriter, he wrote special material for nightclub entertainers and dance bands. He worked as a violinist in vaudeville house orchestras, and then formed a band in conjunction with composer Saul Chaplin. Cahn was 24 years old when he and Chaplin adapted a Jewish popular song for a new trio known as the Andrew Sisters. The result was "Bei Mir Bist Du Schon," which elevated Patty, Maxine, and LaVerne into the ranks of top recording artists. Such hits as "If It's the Last Thing I Do," "Dedicated to You," "Please Be Kind," "Joseph, Joseph," and "I Want My Share of Love" followed providing Cahn with the reputation that led to a contract with Warner Brothers.

Sammy Cahn's songs were used in only one of Warner's feature films, *Ladies Must Live* (1940). He fared better with both Columbia and Universal which included his work in such low-budget films as *Argentine Nights*, *Time Out for Rhythm*, *Honolulu Lu*, and *Two Latins from Manhattan*. The turning point in Cahn's Hollywood career came in 1942 when he collaborated with Jule Styne on the number "I've Heard That Song Before" for Republic's *Youth on Parade*. The song reached the top of "Your Hit Parade" and was nominated for the Oscar. Cahn's second bid from the Academy came two years later for the "Hit Parade" leader "I'll Walk Alone" from Universal's 1944 musical *Follow the Boys*. Cahn's popular film songs during World War II included "There Goes That Song Again," "I Should Care," and "Come Out, Come Out, Wherever You Are." During that same period, Cahn's "I Fall in Love Too Easily" and "Anywhere" competed as the Best Song of 1945

Sammy Cahn supplied the words for Oscar nominees introduced by two of the biggest stars to emerge in post-war Hollywood. Doris Day sang "It's Magic" in *Romance on the High Seas* (1948) and the title song for *It's a Great Feeling* (1949), and Mario Lanza sang "Be My Love" in *The Toast of New Orleans* (1950) and the title song for *Because You're Mine* (1952). Jane Powell introduced still another of Cahn's Best Song contenders,

"Wonder Why?" in the 1951 release *Rich, Young and Pretty*. In 1953, he entered the financial end of the film industry when he produced *3 Sailors and a Girl* for Warner Brothers.

After nine chances at Hollywood's highest honor, Sammy Cahn took home the 1954 Oscar for the title song "Three Coins in the Fountain." The lyricist's collaborator on the winning song, Jule Styne, had abandoned motion pictures for the New York stage, and Cahn had begun working with composer James Van Heusen. Within eight years, the team had collected three Academy Awards for "All the Way" from *The Joker Is Wild* (1957), "High Hopes" from *A Hole in the Head* (1959), and "Call Me Irresponsible" from *Papa's Delicate Condition* (1963).

The film star most closely associated with the lyrics of Sammy Cahn is Frank Sinatra with whom Cahn began working when the singer was with the Tommy Dorsey Orchestra in the late thirties. Cahn has written songs for almost a dozen films starring Sinatra. Other screen favorites for whom the lyricist has created are Barbara Stanwyck, Rita Hayworth, Nelson Eddy, Gene Kelly, Betty Hutton, Danny Kaye, Betty Grable, Bing Crosby, Marilyn Monroe, Dean Martin, and Julie Andrews. His songs nominated for Academy Awards also include "I'll Never Stop Loving You" (1955), "(Love Is) The Tender Trap" (1955), "Written on the Wind" (1956), "To Love and Be Loved" (1958), "The Best of Everything" (1959), "The Second Time Around" (1960), "Pocketful of Miracles" (1961), "My Kind of Town" (1964), "Where Love Has Gone" (1964), "Thoroughly Modern Millie" (1967), "Star!" (1968), "All That Love Went to Waste" (1973), and "Now That We're in Love" (1975).

In 1974, Sammy Cahn appeared on Broadway in a presentation of his own songs titled *Words and Music*. The show was also successfully staged in London and several major cities in the United States. The year of his Broadway debut saw the publication of his autobiography *I Should Care*. He was featured in a segment about motion picture songwriters in the 1976 film *That's Entertainment, Part II*.

Cahn's avocation is writing lyrics on request for special occasions, such as the birthday of the president of a national chain of fast-food restaurants. He generally undertakes this work purely as a labor of love. He's also president of the Songwriters' Hall of Fame—a New York–based organization devoted to honoring the nation's foremost songwriters and preserving their memorabilia in its archives.

At the age of 66, Samy Cahn remains one of the busiest men in the music profession.

1940	LADIES MUST LIVE	I Could Make You Care
	ARGENTINE NIGHTS	Amigo, We Go Riding Tonight
		The Dowry Song
		Once upon a Dream
		Argentine Nights
1941	TIME OUT FOR RHYTHM	As If You Didn't Know
		Twiddlin' My Thumbs
		Did Anyone Ever Tell You?
		Boogie Woogie Man
		Time Out for Rhythm
		Obviously, the Gentleman Prefers to Dance
		The Rio de Janeiro
		Shows How Wrong a Gal Can Be
	GO WEST, YOUNG LADY	Somewhere along the Trail
		Go West, Young Lady
		Most Gentlemen Don't Prefer a Lady
		I Wish I Could Be a Singing Cowboy
		Doggie, Take Your Time
		Rise to Arms
	SING FOR YOUR SUPPER	Why Is It So?
	ROOKIES ON PARADE	The Army Builds Men
		I Love You More
		Mother Never Told Me Why
		My Kinda Love
		You'll Never Get Rich
		What More Do You Want?
		My Kinda Music
	TWO LATINS FROM MANHATTAN	How Do You Say It?
		The Kid with the Drum
	HONOLULU LU	That's the Kind of Work I Do
		Honolulu Lu

1942	YOUTH ON PARADE	I've Heard That Song Before
		You're So Good to Me
	TWO YANKS IN TRINIDAD	Trinidad
	JOHNNY DOUGHBOY	Baby's a Big Girl Now
		All Done, All Through
		It Takes a Guy Like I
		Victory Caravan
	BLONDIE GOES TO COLLEGE	Do I Need You?
		Loyal Sons of Leighton
	BLONDIE'S BLESSED EVENT	Ah Loo Loo
1943	CRAZY HOUSE	I Ought to Dance
	LET'S FACE IT	Plain Jane Doe
		Who Did? I Did, Yes I Did
	THUMBS UP	From Here on In
		Love Is a Corny Thing
		Who Are the British?
	LADY OF BURLESQUE	So This Is You
		Take It Off the E String
	THE HEAT'S ON	Thinkin' about the Wabash
1944	FOLLOW THE BOYS	I'll Walk Alone
		A Better Day Is Coming
	JAM SESSION	Vict'ry Polka
	CAROLINA BLUES	There Goes That Song Again
		Mister Beebe
		Poor Little Rhode Island
		You Make Me Dream Too Much
		Thanks a Lot
	STEP LIVELY	Come Out, Come Out, Wherever You Are
		And Then You Kissed Me
		Where Does Love Begin?
		Some Other Time
		Ask the Madam
		As Long as There's Music
		Why Must There Be an Op'ning Song?

	KNICKERBOCKER
	HOLIDAY
		Love Has Made This Such a
		  Lovely Day
		One More Smile
				TARS AND SPARS	I'm Glad I Waited for You
					Kiss Me Hello
					Love Is a Merry-Go-Round
					He's a Hero
					I Love Eggs
					After the War, Baby
					I Have a Love in Every
					  Port
					When I Get to Town
					Don't Call on Me
					I Always Meant to Tell You

	JANIE	Keep Your Powder Dry			
1945	ANCHORS AWEIGH	I Fall in Love Too Easily The Charm of You I Begged Her What Makes the Sunset? We Hate to Leave			

	TONIGHT AND EVERY
	NIGHT
		Anywhere
		Cry and You Cry Alone
		The Heart of a City
		Tonight and Every Night
		What Does an English Girl
		  Think of a Yank?
		The Boy I Left Behind
		You Excite Me
				THE KID FROM
				BROOKLYN
					I Love an Old-Fashioned
					  Song
					You're the Cause of It All
					Hey, What's Your Name?
					Josie
					Sunflower Song
					Pavlova

	THRILL OF A ROMANCE	I Should Care	1947	IT HAPPENED IN BROOKLYN	Time after Time It's the Same Old Dream I Believe The Brooklyn Bridge Whose Baby Are You? The Song's Gotta Come from the Heart
	THE STORK CLUB	Love Me			
	A SONG TO REMEMBER	A Song to Remember			

1946	CINDERELLA JONES	When the One You Love
		  Simply Won't Love Back
		If You're Waitin', I'm
		  Waitin', Too
		Cinderella Jones
		You Never Know Where
		  You're Goin' Till You
		  Get There
		Our Theme
				LADIES' MAN	What Am I Gonna Do about
					  You?
					I Gotta Gal I Love
					Away Out West
					I'm as Ready as I'll Ever Be

	EARL CARROLL'S
	SKETCH BOOK
		I've Never Forgotten
		The Lady with a Mop
		Oh, Henry!
		What Makes You Beautiful,
		  Beautiful?
		I Was Silly, I Was
		  Headstrong, I Was
		  Impetuous
		We Met over a Bottle of
		  Vino
		Salvo
			1948	ROMANCE ON THE HIGH
				SEAS
					It's Magic
					Put 'em in a Box
					It's You or No One
					I'm in Love
					The Tourist Trade
					Run, Run, Run
					Two Lovers Met in the
					  Night

	SWEETHEART OF SIGMA CHI	Five Minutes More			

TWO GUYS FROM TEXAS	Every Day I Love You	
	I Don't Care If It Rains All Night	
	Hankerin'	
	There's Music in the Land	
	I Never Met a Texan	
	I Wanna Be a Cowboy in the Movies	
	At the Rodeo	
SONS OF ADVENTURE	If It's Love	
MIRACLE OF THE BELLS	Ever Homeward	

1949 IT'S A GREAT FEELING
- It's a Great Feeling
- Fiddle Dee Dee
- That Was a Big Fat Lie
- Blame My Absent-Minded Heart
- At the Cafe Rendezvous
- There's Nothin' Rougher Than Love
- Give Me a Song with a Beautiful Melody

ALWAYS LEAVE THEM LAUGHING
- You're Too Intense
- Always Leave Them Laughing
- Say Farewell
- Clink Your Glasses
- The Wonder of It All

1950 YOUNG MAN WITH A HORN
- Melancholy Rhapsody

THE TOAST OF NEW ORLEANS
- Be My Love
- I'll Never Love You
- The Bayou Lullaby
- Boom Biddy Boom Boom
- The Tina-Lina
- The Toast of New Orleans

THE WEST POINT STORY
- Ten Thousand Four Hundred and Thirty-Two Sheep
- By the Kissing Rock
- You Love Me
- Military Polka
- Long Before I Knew You
- It Could Only Happen in Brooklyn
- The Corps

BORDERLINE
- Carlotta

1951 RICH, YOUNG AND PRETTY
- Wonder Why
- Dark Is the Night
- I Can See You
- We Never Talk Much
- How D'ya Like Your Eggs in the Morning?
- Tonight for Sure
- Paris
- C'est Fini

SUGARFOOT
- Oh! He Looked Like He Might Buy the Wine

TWO TICKETS TO BROADWAY
- Let's Make Comparisons

DOUBLE DYNAMITE
- It's Only Money
- Kisses and Tears

1952 BECAUSE YOU'RE MINE
- Because You're Mine

APRIL IN PARIS
- The Diff'rence
- It Must Be Good
- I'm Gonna Ring the Bell Tonight
- Give Me Your Lips
- I Know a Place
- I Ask You
- Who Needs It?
- That's What Makes Paris Paree
- Life Is Such a Pleasure

SHE'S WORKING HER WAY THROUGH COLLEGE
- I'll Be Loving You
- The Stuff That Dreams Are Made Of
- Give 'em What They Want
- Love Is Still for Free

1953	3 SAILORS AND A GIRL	Face to Face
		Home Is Where the Heart Is
		You're but Oh So Right
		Kiss Me or I'll Scream
		The Lately Song
		I Made Myself a Promise
		There Must Be a Reason
		When It's Love
		Show Me a Happy Woman and I'll Show You a Mis'rable Man
		My Heart Is a Singing Heart
	PETER PAN	Second Star to the Right
		You Can Fly, You Can Fly, You Can Fly
		What Made the Red Man Red?
		Your Mother and Mine
		The Elegant Captain Hook
1954	THREE COINS IN THE FOUNTAIN	Three Coins in the Fountain
	INDISCRETION OF AN AMERICAN WIFE	Autumn in Rome
		Indiscretion
	CHANGE OF HEART	If It's Love
	A WOMAN'S WORLD	It's a Woman's World
	VERA CRUZ	Vera Cruz
1955	LOVE ME OR LEAVE ME	I'll Never Stop Loving You
	THE TENDER TRAP	(Love Is) The Tender Trap
	PETE KELLY'S BLUES	Pete Kelly's Blues
	QUINCANNON, FRONTIER SCOUT	Quincannon, Frontier Scout
	YOU'RE NEVER TOO YOUNG	You're Never Too Young
		I Know Your Mother Loves You
		Love Is All That Matters
		Simpatico
		Face the Music
		Relax-ay-voo
		I Like to Hike

	HOW TO BE VERY, VERY POPULAR	How to Be Very, Very Popular
	AIN'T MISBEHAVIN'	I Love That Rickey Tickey Tickey
	THE SEVEN YEAR ITCH	The Girl Upstairs
		The Seven Year Itch
1956	WRITTEN ON THE WIND	Written on the Wind
	SOMEBODY UP THERE LIKES ME	Somebody Up There Likes Me
	FOREVER DARLING	Forever Darling
	MEET ME IN LAS VEGAS	Hell Hath No Fury
		If You Can Dream
		My Lucky Charm
		The Gal with the Yaller Shoes
		I Refuse to Rock 'n' Roll
		Everytime We Meet
		You Got Looks
		If You've Never Been to Vegas
		It's Fun to Be in Love
		Meet Me in Las Vegas
	THE OPPOSITE SEX	The Opposite Sex
		Now, Baby, Now
		Dere's Yellow Gold on da Trees
		The Rock and Roll Tumbleweed
		A Perfect Love
		Jungle Red
		Mosey
	SERENADE	Serenade
		My Destiny

	ANYTHING GOES	A Second Hand Turban and a Crystal Ball	
		Ya Gotta Give the People Hoke	
		You Can Bounce Right Back	
	THE COURT JESTER	Life Could Not Better Be	
		Baby, Let Me Take You Dreaming	
		Out Fox the Fox	
		My Heart Knows a Lovely Song	
		I Live to Love	
		Pass the Basket	
		Where Walks My True Love	
		The Maladjusted Jester	
	PARDNERS	Wind, the Wind	
		Me 'n' You 'n' the Moon	
		Pardners	
		Buckskin Beauty	
		The Test of Time	
1957	THE JOKER IS WILD	All the Way	
	UNTIL THEY SAIL	Until They Sail	
	DON'T GO NEAR THE WATER	Don't Go Near the Water	
	TEN THOUSAND BEDROOMS	Ten Thousand Bedrooms	
		Only Trust Your Heart	
		You I Love	
		Money Is a Problem	
	THIS COULD BE THE NIGHT	This Could Be the Night	
	BEAU JAMES	His Honor, the Mayor of New York	

1958	SOME CAME RUNNING	To Love and Be Loved
	THE LONG HOT SUMMER	The Long Hot Summer
		Hey, Eula
	INDISCREET	Indiscreet
	HOME BEFORE DARK	Home Before Dark
	ROCK-A-BYE BABY	Dormi, Dormi, Dormi
		Rock-a-Bye Baby
		Why Can't He Care for Me?
		Love Is a Lonely Thing
		The White Virgin of the Nile
		The Land of La La La
	THE SOUND AND THE FURY	The Sound and the Fury
	UP IN LIGHTS	Sounds in the Night
	PARTY GIRL	Party Girl
	PARIS HOLIDAY	Life Is for Lovin'
		Love Won't Let You Get Away
		Nothing in Common
	ANNA LUCASTA	That's Anna
	KINGS GO FORTH	Monique

1959	A HOLE IN THE HEAD	High Hopes All My Tomorrows		WAKE ME WHEN IT'S OVER	Wake Me When It's Over
	BEST OF EVERYTHING	The Best of Everything		LET'S MAKE LOVE	Incurably Romantic Let's Make Love Specialization Hey, You with the Crazy Eyes
	THEY CAME TO CORDURA	They Came to Cordura			
	THIS EARTH IS MINE	This Earth Is Mine		OCEAN'S 11	Ain't That a Kick in the Head? Ee-o Eleven
	SAY ONE FOR ME	Say One for Me You Can't Love 'em All Chico's Choo-Choo The Secret of Christmas The Night That Rock 'n' Roll Died (Almost) You're Starting to Get to Me I Couldn't Care Less The Girl Most Likely to Suceed		THE WORLD OF SUZIE WONG	Suzie Wong
				WHO WAS THAT LADY?	Who Was That Lady?
			1961	POCKETFUL OF MIRACLES	Pocketful of Miracles
				BY LOVE POSSESSED	By Love Possessed
				THE PLEASURE OF HIS COMPANY	Pleasure of His Company
	CAREER	(Love Is a) Career	1962	HOW THE WEST WAS WON	Home in the Meadow
	JOURNEY TO THE CENTER OF THE EARTH	Twice as Tall The Faithful Heart Come Spring I'm Never Alone		BOYS' NIGHT OUT	The Boys' Night Out Cathy
				ROAD TO HONG KONG	Warmer Than a Whisper Teamwork Let's Not Be Sensible The Road to Hong Kong The Only Way to Travel
	NIGHT OF THE QUARTER MOON	Night of the Quarter Moon			
	HOLIDAY FOR LOVERS	Holiday for Lovers		GIGOT	Allo, Allo, Allo Gigot
1960	HIGH TIME	The Second Time Around Nobody's Perfect Showmanship Go! Go! Go!	1963	PAPA'S DELICATE CONDITION	Call Me Irresponsible

	MY SIX LOVES	It's a Darn Good Thing My Six Loves
	COME BLOW YOUR HORN	Come Blow Your Horn The Look of Love
	4 FOR TEXAS	Four for Texas
	UNDER THE YUM YUM TREE	Under the Yum Yum Tree
	JOHNNY COOL	The Ballad of Johnny Cool
1964	ROBIN AND THE 7 HOODS	My Kind of Town ✓ Style I Like to Lead When I Dance All for One and One for All Mister Booze Charlotte Couldn't Charleston Any Man Who Loves His Mother Don't Be a Do-Badder Bang-Bang Give Praise, Give Praise, Give Praise
	WHERE LOVE HAS GONE	Where Love Has Gone ✓
	HONEYMOON HOTEL	Honeymoon Hotel
	THE PLEASURE SEEKERS	Everything Makes Music When You're in Love Costa del Sol
1965	THE SECOND BEST SECRET AGENT IN THE WHOLE WIDE WORLD	The Second Best Secret Agent in the Whole Wide World
1967	THOROUGHLY MODERN MILLIE	Thoroughly Modern Millie The Tapioca
	THE BOBO	Imagine Blue Matador The Bobo
1968	STAR!	Star!
	A FLEA IN HER EAR	A Flea in Her Ear
	THE ODD COUPLE	Tomatoes
	BANDOLERO	There's Got to Be a Better Way
1969	THE GREAT BANK ROBBERY	Rainbow Rider Heaven Helps Him Who Helps Himself
1973	A TOUCH OF CLASS	All That Love Went to Waste I Always Knew Nudge Me Every Morning A Touch of Class
	THE HEARTBREAK KID	Don't Ask Me Why
1975	WHIFFS	Now That We're in Love
	PAPER TIGER	My Little Friend
1976	I WILL, I WILL . . . FOR NOW	I Will, I Will . . . for Now If We Try
	THE DUCHESS AND THE DIRWATER FOX	Lemondrops, Lollipops and Sunbeams
1978	FINGERS	Now Is Forever
	THE STUD	Almost It's Good

The Tender Trap (Metro-Goldwyn-Mayer, 1955).
Collectors Book Store, Hollywood, CA.

Jay Livingston & Ray Evans

Jay Livingston and Ray Evans

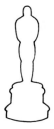

The last of the great songwriters of Hollywood began their motion picture careers near the end of World War II. They were the team of Jay Livingston and Ray Evans. Livingston is the composer in the partnership, and both men write lyrics. They were both born in 1915—Livingston in McDonald, Pennsylvania, and Evans in Salamanca, New York. When both were undergraduates at the University of Pennsylvania, Livingston formed a dance band in which Evans played the saxophone and clarinet. They also filled engagements with orchestras playing on steamships and in cabarets. Comedian Ole Olsen provided the inspiration for their first hit song "G'bye Now" and included the number in the Broadway revue *Hellzapoppin'* in the early 1940s. Livingston served with the Armed Forces during World War II, and Evans was employed by an aircraft company.

The songs of Livingston and Evans were first heard by movie audiences in the Producers Releasing Corporation films *I Accuse My Parents* and *Swing Hostess* released in 1944. The next year, the still unknown team received an Oscar nomination for "The Cat and the Canary" featured in *Why Girls Leave Home*. Livingston and Evans were signed by Paramount, which had been the starting point for more top songwriting talent than any other studio in Hollywood. The first major star to introduce their numbers was Betty Hutton who belted "A Square in the Social Circle" in *The Stork Club* (1945). The team's title song for *Golden Earrings* (1947) and "Buttons and Bows" from *The Paleface* (1948) both became number one on "Your Hit Parade." "Buttons and Bows" won Livingston and Evans their first Academy Award. Two years later, the Academy again bestowed the industry's highest honor on the two songwriters for "Mona Lisa" from *Captain Carey, U.S.A.*

In 1954, the team wrote the score for the experimental musical *Red Garters*—a tongue-in-cheek western entirely photographed against stylized settings. Among the last projects under their Paramount contract was Alfred Hitchcock's *The Man Who Knew Too Much*, in which Doris Day sang the Best Song of 1956, "Whatever Will Be, Will Be (Que Sera, Sera)." It was the fourth of their compositions to lead "Your Hit Parade," and "Tammy" became their fifth number one song.

Jay Livingston and Ray Evans received additional Oscar nominations for "Tammy" from *Tammy and the Bachelor* (1957), "Almost in Your Arms" from *Houseboat* (1958), and the title song "Dear Heart" (1964). Since leaving Paramount, the team has free-lanced and frequently writes lyrics only for the melodies of other composers.

One of the songs played every year at the opening of the film capital's Santa Claus Lane is Livingston and Evans' "Silver Bells." The song was introduced in the motion picture *The Lemon Drop Kid* in 1951. That year, dozens of motion picture stars appeared in the parade down Hollywood Boulevard. The annual Christmas attraction is now dominated by personalities from television.

1944	I ACCUSE MY PARENTS	Are You Happy in Your Work? Love Came between Us Where Can You Be?		WHISPERING SMITH	Laramie
				DREAM GIRL	Dream Girl Drunk with Love
	SWING HOSTESS	Highway Polka Say It with Love Music in My Heart I'll Eat My Hat Let's Capture This Moment I've Got an Invitation		THE SAINTED SISTERS	Please Put Out the Light
				MY OWN TRUE LOVE	My Own True Love
			1949	SORROWFUL JONES	Havin' a Wonderful Wish Rock-a-Bye Bangtail
	PEOPLE ARE FUNNY	Hey, Jose		MY FRIEND IRMA	Here's to Love Just for Fun My One, My Only, My All
1945	ON STAGE EVERYBODY	Stuff Like That There		THE GREAT LOVER	A Thousand Violins Lucky Us
	THE STORK CLUB	A Square in the Social Circle			
	WHY GIRLS LEAVE HOME	The Cat and the Canary What Am I Saying? Call Me		SONG OF SURRENDER	Song of Surrender
				STREETS OF LAREDO	Streets of Laredo
	CRIME, INC.	I'm Guilty Lonesome Little Camera Girl		BRIDE OF VENGEANCE	Give Thy Love
			1950	CAPTAIN CAREY, U.S.A.	Mona Lisa
1946	MONSIEUR BEAUCAIRE	Warm as Wine A Coach and Four We'll Drink Every Drop in the Shop		COPPER CANYON	Copper Canyon
				MY FRIEND IRMA GOES WEST	I'll Always Love You Baby, Obey Me Fiddle and Gittar Band
1947	GOLDEN EARRINGS	Golden Earrings		THE FURIES	T. C. Roundup Time
	THE IMPERFECT LADY	Piccadilly Tilly		PAID IN FULL	You're Wonderful
	MY FAVORITE BRUNETTE	Beside You		FANCY PANTS	Home Cookin' Fancy Pants Yes, M'lord
1948	THE PALEFACE	Buttons and Bows Meetcha 'Round the Corner		THE REDHEAD AND THE COWBOY	Trav'lin' Free
	ISN'T IT ROMANTIC?	Wond'rin' When I Shoulda Quit When I Was Ahead Miss Julie July Indiana Dinner At the Nickelodeon	1951	HERE COMES THE GROOM	Bonne Nuit Misto Cristofo Columbo Your Own Little House
				THE LEMON DROP KID	Silver Bells It Doesn't Cost a Dime to Dream They Obviously Want Me to Sing

AARON SLICK FROM PUNKIN CRICK	Life Is a Beautiful Thing	
	Why Should I Believe in Love?	
	Marshmallow Moon	
	My Beloved	
	I'd Like to Baby You	
	Purt Nigh, but Not Plumb	
	Still Water	
	Chores	
	Saturday Night in Punkin Crick	
	The General Store	
	Will You Be at Home in Heaven?	
	Step Right Up	
	Soda Shop	
	The Spider and the Fly	
MY FAVORITE SPY	Just a Moment More	
RHUBARB	It's a Privilege to Live in Brooklyn	
	Friendly Finance Company	
THE BIG CARNIVAL	We're Coming, Leo	
CROSSWINDS	Crosswinds	
THAT'S MY BOY	Ridgeville Fight Song	

1952 | SOMEBODY LOVES ME | Love Him
| | Thanks to You
| | Honey, Oh My Honey

| WHAT PRICE GLORY? | My Love, My Life
| | You and Me Together

| SON OF PALEFACE | California Rose
| | Wing Ding Tonight!
| | What a Dirty Shame

| ANYTHING CAN HAPPEN | Love Laughs at Kings

1953 | THUNDER IN THE EAST | The Ruby and the Pearl

| THE STARS ARE SINGING | Haven't Got a Worry
| | Lovely Weather for Ducks
| | My Kind of Day
| | I Do, I Do, I Do
| | My Heart Is Home

| OFF LIMITS | Right or Wrong
| | All about Love
| | The Military Policeman

| HERE COME THE GIRLS | When You Love Someone
| | Girls!
| | Ya Got Class!
| | Never So Beautiful
| | Heavenly Days
| | At the Circus
| | Ali Baba
| | It's Torment

| THOSE REDHEADS FROM SEATTLE | Mr. Banjo Man

| CASANOVA'S BIG NIGHT | Pretty Mandolin (Tic-a-tic-a-tic)

1954 | RED GARTERS | Red Garters
| | Meet a Happy Guy
| | A Dime and a Dollar
| | Brave Man
| | This Is Greater Than I Thought
| | Good Intentions
| | Bad News
| | Man and Woman
| | The Robin Randall Song
| | Lady Killer
| | Vaquero

| MISTER ROBERTS | Let Me Hear You Whisper

1955 | THREE RING CIRCUS | Hey, Punchinello

| THE SECOND GREATEST SEX | The Second Greatest Sex

| LUCY GALLANT | How Can I Tell Her?

1956 | THE MAN WHO KNEW TOO MUCH | Whatever Will Be, Will Be (Que Sera, Sera)
| | We'll Love Again

| ISTANBUL | I Was a Little Too Lonely

| THE SCARLET HOUR | Never Let Me Go

1957	TAMMY AND THE BACHELOR	Tammy
	VERTIGO	Vertigo
	THREE LITTLE BEARS	Three Little Bears
	THE JAMES DEAN STORY	Let Me Be Loved
	RAW WIND IN EDEN	The Magic Touch
	THE LIFE, LOVES AND ADVENTURES OF OMAR KHAYYAM	Tell My Love Loves of Omar Khayyam
	THE BIG BEAT	As I Love You I Waited So Long
1958	HOUSEBOAT	Almost in Your Arms Bing! Bang! Bong!
	ANOTHER TIME, ANOTHER PLACE	Another Time, Another Place
	SADDLE THE WIND	Saddle the Wind
	THIS HAPPY FEELING	This Happy Feeling
	ONCE UPON A HORSE	Once upon a Horse
1959	A PRIVATE'S AFFAIR	Warm and Willing 36-24-36 The Same Old Army
	TAKE A GIANT STEP	Take a Giant Step
	THE BLUE ANGEL	Lola-Lola
1961	ALL HANDS ON DECK	I Got It Made Somewhere There's Home There's No One like You All Hands on Deck
1964	DEAR HEART	Dear Heart
1965	HARLOW	Lonely Girl
	NEVER TOO LATE	Never Too Late
	THE THIRD DAY	Love Me Now
1966	THIS PROPERTY IS CONDEMNED	Wish Me a Rainbow
	WHAT DID YOU DO IN THE WAR, DADDY?	In the Arms of Love
	TORN CURTAIN	Green Years
	THE NIGHT OF THE GRIZZLY	Angela
1967	WAIT UNTIL DARK	Wait until Dark
1974	LOVE IS FOREVER	Love Is Forever
1976	FOX TROT	Fox Trot

Red Garters (Paramount, 1954).
Collectors Book Store, Hollywood, CA.

Film Songs

264

272

Z

Films

People